HOW TO TALK TO PEOPLE

(AND NOT FEEL LIKE AN IDIOT)

A. MICHAEL RICHARDS

BOREALIS
BOOKS

CONTENTS

HOW TO TALK TO PEOPLE

(AND NOT FEEL LIKE AN IDIOT

The Communication Skills You Need to
Cut Through Social Anxiety, Connect With Anyone,
and Spark Engaging Conversations

contained within this document, including, but not limited to, errors, omissions, or inaccuracies.

INTRODUCTION

Communication is the solvent of all problems
and is the foundation for personal development.
– Peter Shepherd

Communication is the most vital tool in any human being's arsenal. We rely on it to express our feelings, share our experiences, and connect with those around us. As useful as communication is, though, it can often be a very frustrating thing. Sometimes we have trouble conveying the things we want to explain properly. "It's on the tip of my tongue," we say, and yet the words we are grasping for seem to fail us. Other times it feels like we've become some bizarre parody of the three wise monkeys. One of us is covering our mouths, one of us is covering our eyes, and yet another covers our ears, throwing one obstacle after another in our path. As we parody the three monkeys, we lose our ability to communicate with each other properly. Understandably, we get frustrated, humiliated, or even angry that we're not being heard. Perhaps we end up getting into an argument as a result. Perhaps we end up saying something cringe-worthy, awkward, or embarrassing—at least to us. Afterward, we hang our heads every time we remember what we said. "Why did I have to *say* that?" we wonder as heat floods our cheeks. "I feel so stupid!" Or possibly the worst feeling of all— not having anything to say whatsoever, leaving the person standing in front of us feeling confused and uncomfortable. The dialog comes so much easier to us later on, when we're rehashing the conversation in the shower, but in that moment when we're face-to-face in conversation, your mind is blank.

The thing is, everyone experiences each of these scenarios from time to time. Everyone has trouble communicating; some are just more aware of their struggle than others. Communication is a form of art, after all, and it's one that can be very difficult to master. This is because there are many nuances to communication. How you talk to your best friends, for example, is bound to be very different from how you talk to your mother or boss. Talking to strangers can be challenging as well. This is doubly true for those of us who are more introverted by nature—in that we feel more comfortable carrying conversations in our heads than with other people. A lot of people find talking to and getting to know new people to be a little intimidating. They feel like they're fumbling through the conversation and perhaps end up quieting down for fear of embarrassing themselves. As a result, they find forming new friendships and connections to be a little difficult. Some people, though, struggle with a great deal of anxiety when they even think about talking to others. The fear of ruining an opportunity or making a matter worse can be paralyzing. Often, they feel like they'll be misunderstood by others, struggle to find the right words to express what they mean, grow even more embarrassed and flustered, or find some other clever way to make a fool of themselves.

Sound familiar? If so, you are not alone. Take heart! Having the knowledge and tools you need to calm some of those fears can go a long way in helping you make great progress in this area. We'll examine the most common communication obstacles and work through what you can do about them. We'll walk through a conversation from beginning to end and think through potential pitfalls. You'll learn what you need to approach conversations of all kinds without overthinking things like your body language or tone as you gain confidence. From there, you'll be able to develop meaningful, lasting relationships, whether with friends, family, or maybe even a significant other. Some of what you'll read may seem overly simple, but oftentimes we struggle with the simple things until we've taken the time to think through them and recognize how they can be implemented in daily life.

These, of course, sound like bold claims. I can almost hear you asking, "What makes you so sure you can help me with all this?" The short answer is. personal experience. As a counselor, I've helped countless people overcome many types of personal and emotional struggles. As a kid, though, I was incredibly shy and never willingly spoke up in front of others. I had a hard time getting to know new people and was conveniently "sick" whenever it was time for any kind of public speaking or group collaboration. Today though, I have turned all of that around. Aside from being a counselor—someone who has to confidently talk to other people to be able to do his job—I'm also a public speaker. Given how far I've come and how much I've changed over the years, I know exactly what you're going through. I also know what you can do to gain the confidence you need to start talking and forming deep connections with others. As I thrive on helping others, helping you overcome daunting things, like imposter syndrome, social anxiety, and feelings of incompetence, matters greatly to me. So, are you ready to begin?

SECTION ONE

Taking the Right Approach

without scaring them off

CHAPTER 1
YOUR MINDSET

Why do I psych myself out before I start?

G etting to know new people can be a scary undertaking, but only if you allow it to be in your mind. If there's one thing I could convince you of, I would want it to be that the task of talking to people is not as daunting as it seems. Wait! Don't toss the book in the trash just yet; hear me out. If you could step out of your mind for just a moment before a conversation and get a glimpse inside the other person's mind, chances are, you would find that it is full of the very same fears that you have, and you would feel more compassion than fear. You would likely be put at ease knowing that they are judging themselves more than they're judging you. Sure, that isn't the case with everyone you'll meet. There will always be people ready to give you an eye roll or rude remark, but those people are who they are. You're not going to be able to change who they are by employing the perfect conversation skills, and they likely aren't the people you want to build connections with, anyway. In these cases, accept the eye rolls and negativity as the cost of doing business with a negative individual, and move on. Do not take it as a mark against yourself. This can be difficult to remember, but very important, as these types of interactions can leave you thinking that the problem is yourself and intimidate you away from engaging more of the right people.

In addition to the general population being less intimidating than you might think, most of the time, the stakes of social interactions are not as high as they seem. Unless you're being interviewed for a top position in a cutthroat line of work, the people you're talking to are probably much more compassionate and understanding than you might imagine. It feels as though making one wrong move will leave a lasting bad impression that will doom any opportunity before it starts. But in reality, it's often not the first impression or the mistake that dooms a relationship, but rather, it's not knowing what to do *after* the mistake that's the problem. Or worse, being too afraid to have the interaction in the first place.

The way you think about yourself, others, and how you believe others perceive you will have a significant impact on how you behave around them. If you're nervous when you're approaching people and let your fearful questions guide your actions— what will I say? What will they think?— then you'll find starting a conversation with them difficult. How could you not, with the number of negative questions and feelings you're battling while you're trying to introduce yourself? On the flip side, if you manage to change your approach and you're a little more confi-dent, you'll have a much easier time connecting with others. This is easier said than done, of course. But it's not impossible.

The trick to being able to manage it is identifying what's holding you back. What's making you so nervous and damaging your confidence so much that you hesitate when talking to other people? Usually, there is one of four culprits responsible for this. These are a fixed mindset, imposter syndrome, having a defeatist attitude, and believing you have nothing valuable to contribute. Let's look at how each can play a role in psyching yourself out.

FIXED MINDSET

More often than not, when people have an ongoing fear of interacting with others, something that happened much earlier in their lives convinced them that it's better if they just don't interact at all. Do you remember a time like that? For many of us, it was some embarrassing moment years ago— even as a young child— that can still make us cringe to think about it. The problem with embarrassments happening at a young age is that you are still devel-oping who you believe you are as a person. When you put yourself out there and get embarrassed in the process, this can develop a lifelong insecurity believing you will always get the same results if you ever put yourself out there in that way again. Without the maturity to understand that— hey, embarrassing things happen to everybody, just laugh at it and learn from it— a young person is more likely to "learn" instead that they're a person who says dumb things, gets laughed at, or hurts people's feelings. Of course, that isn't an accurate or fair assessment, but they believe it nonetheless, and if they're not careful, it can become part of their identity.

Sound extreme? Think back to middle school. Let's say you're the new kid in class. You don't know anybody in your new school but would like to make friends. You go into the lunchroom and look around for a table to sit at. There, in the corner, is a mostly empty table where a couple of other students are talking. They look interesting, and you'd like to walk up to that table and sit down, maybe introduce yourself. But perhaps they took one look at you and told you that you couldn't sit there? Maybe they gathered their stuff and left once you sat down at their table? What if they found you boring or annoying once you start talking to them? Or worse, you embarrassed yourself when you were talking to them, and they made fun of you in front of the crowd?

Likely, one of these things *did* happen to you at

some point because, well, they happen to most of us. We will think back to several possible scenarios that people deal with growing up in hopes that the examples will prompt a memory of your own that you can think back to. Try to think of a specific time. Now imagine if you were to walk into a new group of people today— whether in the break room at a new job or trying to mingle at a party or new workout class. When you consider talking to someone new, what is it that you're afraid of? What if they take one look at you and make it clear that you can't join them? What if they quiet down or move away when you approach? What if you embarrass yourself and you become the new joke at the office?

Do you see how it's the same issue with a different backdrop? For some reason, we believe that if it happened to us once, then that's the type of person we are. I'm awkward. I'm a geek. I'm not good at this. I make people uncomfortable. If those are the thoughts you believe, guess what? You're going to act like an awkward geek who isn't good at things, and you'll make people uncomfortable! But what if you were good at it? How would you approach the situation, then? Imagine you're a suave, confident person with all the necessary skills to accomplish your next task. Imagine how you would look, walk, and speak if that were true. Then DO

THAT. Seem fake? I'm here to tell you that that's precisely what you've been doing all along. You believed you weren't good enough, so you imagined yourself failing and then acted accordingly. Your thoughts have a profound effect on your mind and body, and they shape the way you behave. You have to flip the script going on in your brain.

Growth Mindset is a term coined by Carol Dweck, a psychologist from Stanford University. Her studies are fascinating, but I will summarize them by saying that if a person believes that their skills, or even their capacity to obtain new skills, and understanding can improve over time, they are said to have a *growth mindset*. If, however, they believe deep down that the way they are now is the way they will always be, they have a *fixed mindset*. The participants in Dweck's studies showed that if a person believed they could be different, they became different. And if they believed their personality, intelligence, and abilities, or lack thereof, was part of their DNA and they could never change, they didn't change. The fact is, who you are today— your personality, talents, and even your interests, were not predetermined at birth. They only describe who you are *today*. The age-old question of whether or not a person can change does not need to be debated any longer. Science has already settled it. If you think change is possible, then change is possible. So the real question is: do *you* believe that *you* can change? That is what will determine whether or not you *can* change.

So go back to those early failures in your life, and forgive that inner child who was humiliated or who made a mess of things. Every time you fear a social situation, try to determine what you're afraid of. Did something like that happen before? If not, then determine not to let an irrational fear keep you from moving forward. But if it is a wound from your past that's keeping you from wanting to take this next step, go back there in your mind. Tell that kid what you would say to any other kid— that it's ok to mess things up. It happens to everyone, and it doesn't mean you'll always mess up. It is what you do next that matters, and that isn't controlled by what you did in the past.

IMPOSTER SYNDROME

Have you ever felt like you don't measure up to where you ought to be? (Collective head nods all around.) Of course, you have. This feeling can be compounded into a crippling insecurity, though, when we imagine that in addition to not being as good as you're supposed to be, everyone else *is* as good or better than *they're* supposed to be. When you feel like you have to put on an act to convince people that you deserve to be where you are— whether that's having a certain profession, contributing to a project, or to a conversation— we call it Imposter syndrome. Or just Imposterism, since it really isn't a syndrome, just a state of mind that comes and goes. Imposter Syndrome is something that causes you to believe that you are not as competent, qualified, or "insert adjective here" as other people think you are (Cuncic, 2020). Have you ever read (or been made to read) J.D. Salinger's *The Catcher in the Rye*? If you have, you might recall that its main character, Holden, had this (annoying) habit of calling everyone a phony. Well, imposter syndrome is having an inner Holden Caulfield constantly pointing out how phony *you* are, despite whatever successes you might have achieved.

How can you tell if you have imposter syndrome, then? Well, for one thing, people who deal with imposter syndrome often doubt themselves, even in fields where they excel. Say you're really good at drawing. Your paintings in art class are constantly being praised by your classmates and your professors. But there's a voice in your head that always questions how they would compare to a *real* artist's work. It keeps saying that anyone who sees them will realize what a phony artist you are any day now and change their minds about you.

Three certain signs that you experience Imposter Syndrome are:

• Self-doubt about your worthiness, despite all evidence to the contrary.

• The fear of being "found out" and having others think you're a fake or that you don't belong.

• Negative thoughts that reinforce the idea that you don't belong.

Imposter syndrome can affect you and your communication skills in several ways. First, it can severely impact your confidence level, making it difficult for you to talk and engage with others. Second, the fear of being found out might cause you to avoid interacting with others as much as you can. This can cause you to be a bit of a loner, hanging out on the sidelines rather than joining the fray. The fear of being "found out" and the isolation you subject yourself to can have some unfortunate consequences. It can cause your anxiety levels to spike and remain high continually. You'll constantly be on edge, walking on eggshells so that nobody realizes what a "fraud" you are. Ending up with chronic anxiety in this way often leads to a whole host of health problems, such as headaches, digestive trouble, and a weakened immune system. These can be problematic, to say the least. At the same time, imposter syndrome might lead to depression. How could it not if you're actively avoiding people and social interaction, not to mention the support you both crave and need?

As the old adage goes, the first step to fixing the problem is recognizing there is one. But what if you're unsure whether you have imposter syndrome or not? How can you tell? Simple! You can tell if you have imposter syndrome by asking yourself a few short questions. The key to this technique is to be honest in your answers, even when they make you a little uncomfortable:

- Do you secretly attribute your success to outside factors rather than your hard work or abilities?
- How sensitive are you to constructive criticism? For instance, if your basketball coach were to give you some pointers on how to do a jump shot, would you appreciate it, or would you get upset or angry that you're not "good enough" or worry that the coach doesn't think you should be on the team?
- Do you feel like others might find out that you don't know as much as you're

supposed to unless you keep impressing them?

- Do you downplay your skills, talents, and expertise? For instance, would you be inclined to disagree if someone praised your work and talked about your talent?

Now, again, be honest. How did you answer these questions? Based on them, you should be able to figure out whether you have imposter syndrome. Now, imposter syndrome might be caused by many different things. You could have developed it because you grew up with very controlling or overprotective parents. It could be that your parents were highly critical and seldom praised you. Or maybe the pressure you felt to perform well at school bothered you. Perhaps you don't believe you can succeed in any given situation, or you're a bit of a perfectionist, meaning that unless something is flawless, it's not good enough.

Whatever the cause, fear not! Because imposter syndrome can be overcome. Let's say you took that first step you needed to and recognized you had imposter syndrome. How can you overcome it and take some pressure off yourself?

Start things off by sharing the feelings you have about yourself with others. Sharing how you feel like a phony and are afraid of being found out can be a great way of mitigating those feelings. By doing so, you can air them out and stop them from festering the way an old wound might if the bandage isn't removed after a certain point to let it breathe. By talking about your feelings, you can start to see how irrational they are. You can also get support from people who care about you.

Once you've started talking with others, sit down and make an honest assessment of your skills and abilities. Include everything you've achieved in this assessment. In fact, list them. Write down everything that you're good at, and don't be humble. This is one of those exercises where humility is just not wanted. Once you're finished, take a look at what you've written. Do they really fit in with what you believed about yourself and your abilities till now?

A lot of us tend to compare ourselves to others. It's almost instinctual. Try to notice when you do this and actively get yourself to stop. When you compare yourself to others, you only feed the imposter syndrome fire inside you. Not only that, but you actually pour gasoline onto it and let it rage. Focus on what others tell you in social situations rather than thinking, "I wish I was as good as her at making friends. Look how easily she can just go up to and talk to people she doesn't know. Why can't I do that?" In keeping with that, try to reduce the amount of time you spend on social media. We tend to compare ourselves to people we see online a great deal, and reducing your online time could definitely help with that. Keep in mind that people tend only to allow others to see their best qualities and experiences. That is not the whole story.

Finally, take baby steps. You're not going to vanquish imposter syndrome in a single day like you were some knight slaying a dragon. I mean, the dragon will be killed eventually, but it'll be more of a gradual process. As you endeavor to overcome imposter syndrome, try not to get paralyzed by perfection but rather give yourself permission to complete the task imperfectly. It's alright if there's a typo in your essay. Take baby steps with your communication skills as well. Don't expect to be a master conversationalist overnight. Don't wait until you master all aspects of communication before you use them. Take small steps that you wouldn't have taken before for fear of being "found out." Offer an anecdote to your friends when you're all hanging out together, and speak up just once in class. Once you've managed to take such small steps, reward yourself for them. The steps themselves might be small, but their significance for you is huge.

DEFEATISM

Another reason why some people have trouble starting conversations with others is that they have a defeatist attitude. This is when a person feels defeated before they even start. Think back to your childhood. You're the new kid in school and staring at a table full of classmates. You'd like to walk up and introduce yourself, as they seem pretty cool. Yet as you stand there with your lunch tray in your hands, a small voice in the back of your head says, "They won't want you to sit with them." The more you pay attention to this voice, the louder it'll become, and you'll find yourself thinking, "They won't want to hang out with me anyways," or, "I'll just make a fool of myself if I go over there." So, instead of walking up and introducing yourself, you'll hang your head low and walk to an empty lunch table to eat your food by yourself.

Everyone has defeatist thoughts like this at times. The trick is not to let them affect you. If you give into your defeatist thoughts without challenging them, they'll start dictating your attitude and behavior. You might find yourself passing up on opportunities you might have enjoyed, such as trying out for the basketball team, applying for that job, or even just talking to a stranger.

Like imposter syndrome, defeatism can be caused by a lot of different things. One culprit might be low self-esteem. Another might be negative experiences from the past. If you tried to connect with some of your classmates before and were bullied as a result, then odds are you'll have a defeatist attitude when approaching others. Still, another culprit might be having negative core beliefs about yourself. This means holding onto ideas like, "I ruin everything." The problem with these beliefs is that when you do try to do something like make a new friend, you do so with a defeatist attitude. The person you approached with this attitude doesn't really respond to you or engage with you as a result. You are timid and reserved. Unable to make the connection you wanted to, you think to yourself, "I knew I shouldn't have tried to talk to them. I'm such an idiot." The irony in all this is that you don't even realize that the attitude you walked up to this potential new friend with became the obstacle in your way, causing you to stumble and fall.

The questions to answer are how do you defeat a defeatist attitude? How can you overcome such a thing? The first thing you need to do is stop beating yourself up about past failures and mistakes. We all have this habit of replaying unfortunate incidents and events in our minds. If you fell flat on your face in the school cafeteria, for instance, and everyone laughed at you, you'll likely be replaying what happened in your head many times over. The incident may be on a running loop as you lie in bed trying to go to sleep at night, or it might pop into your mind randomly at school, making you flush with embarrassment all over again. The problem with this habit is that it makes you relive the negative emotions you felt that day. These negative emotions, like embarrassment or shame, keep you back from trying new things, like turning to the person sitting next to you and introducing yourself. This is why you need to stop judging or criticizing yourself about past events. At the very least, you need to stop dwelling on them.

Easier said than done, I know. But just try to take a deep breath every time your mind starts wandering to that time in the cafeteria. "There's nothing I can do to change what happened," you can tell yourself. "I can only move forward. People will forget what happened soon enough anyways. So why should I become so hung up on it?" You can also try to be more compassionate towards yourself whenever the incident pops into your mind. Rather than berate yourself by saying, "I can't believe I was so clumsy," say, "Everyone's clumsy sometimes. I'll just be more careful in the future." If you find this difficult, you can always pretend that the incident happened to someone you care about and talk to yourself the way you would talk to them. You'd be surprised to see just how different your attitude suddenly becomes. What would you say to a friend to whom this happened?

This trick can work with another tactic to beat defeatism: changing how you talk to yourself. Pay close attention to how you talk to yourself in your mind. Are you thinking things like, "I'm such an idiot," "No one wants to be friends with me," or "This will never work?" Become more aware of moments like this. Then, make a conscious effort to change them. Try to replace these negative thoughts with more positive ones. One handy strategy might be replacing absolute words, like "never" and "always," with problem-solving words. Turn "This will never work" to "How can I make this work?" Or "I always fail" to "When have I succeeded, and how can I duplicate that?" You can extend it further by replacing "can't" with "I haven't yet," or you can substitute "I failed" with "This way didn't work, so I can try another way." There are many variations of the story, but it was said of Thomas Edison that he was a slacker in school. His teachers said that he would never amount to anything. After a thousand failed attempts, he finally succeeded in the invention of the lightbulb. When asked by a reporter how it felt to fail 1,000 times, he replied, "I didn't fail 1,000 times. The lightbulb was an invention with 1,000 steps." What a mindset! To see every failure as one step closer to success.

If this is too much of a challenge for you, you can always put such thoughts to the test by asking yourself:

- What is my evidence for thinking this? What is my evidence against this thought? (Be honest when answering this question; otherwise, it won't work!)
- I'm expecting things to turn out a certain way. For example, I expect people to laugh at me if I walk up to them and try to introduce myself. But how else might things go?
- What's the worst thing that could happen? You're holding your tray, staring at the table that you want to introduce yourself to. Ask yourself this question when you hesitate: What *is* the worst thing that could happen? How likely is it that it *will* happen?
- Is thinking this way going to help me? Or will it keep me from getting what I want?

Like with imposter syndrome, defeating defeatism means you need to celebrate small wins and accomplishments. Did you finally start talking a bit to a stranger, even if it was just to talk about the weather? Celebrate the accomplishment and feel proud of yourself. This might be a baby step, but baby steps build over time and increase your confidence, leading to even greater wins and accomplishments.

NOT BELIEVING YOU HAVE ANY VALUE TO ADD

A final reason you may have trouble talking to and connecting with people is that you don't believe you can add any value to the conversation. Let's say you're working on a group project for a college class. Everyone's brainstorming and pitching ideas left and right. Well, everyone except you. You're sitting at your corner of the table, scribbling notes, keeping your head down, and not saying anything. An idea does pop into your head, but you hold yourself back, refusing to let it slip out. Why? Because if it's *your* idea, then it can't possibly be good, right? Wrong! You might, in fact, be sitting on a brilliant idea that might make your group project shine among the others. Yet because you're not sharing it, you're denying yourself the opportunity to find out. You're also denying yourself the opportunity to grow closer with your group members and maybe even strike up some friendships.

Not believing you have anything valuable to add to a group or environment is both a loss for you and for that group or environment. People who have this tendency tend to undervalue themselves. They see little value in themselves and, therefore, see little value in whatever it is they can contribute. This is something that's often seen in people with low self-esteem. (Have you noticed how many of these points keep coming back to self-esteem? Good. Keep that in mind.) They also tend to compare themselves to others a lot. They often think things like, "I wish I were smart like her" or "I wish I could be as athletic as he is." These kinds of comparisons can damage your confidence a great deal. Pretty soon, you might become unable to see yourself clearly. You might start to think that you really don't have anything of value to add when you most certainly do! Don't believe me? Then believe the Dalai Lama. It was he who said, "With realization of one's own potential and self-confidence in one's ability, one can build a better world." This means that you can build a better world if only you learn to see your own value.

So, how can you begin to do this? How can you

start discovering how valuable you truly are? By working on your self-esteem levels, of course. As I mentioned, keep self-esteem in mind. The first thing you can work on to increase your self-esteem is to challenge your negative thoughts and beliefs about yourself. Do you remember those tricks you learned to challenge and change negative thoughts? Like replacing "never" and "always" or negative sentences with more positive ones? Well, that technique can greatly boost your self-esteem, especially if you learn to make a regular practice of it. It's the "fake it till you make it" logic. Repeat something often enough, and you will soon start believing it. This is as true of negative things as it is of positive things. Remember this whenever you start talking negatively to or about yourself.

In keeping with all of that, try to notice when you're comparing yourself to others. When you notice this, make a conscious effort to change your thinking. If you catch yourself comparing yourself to others often when you're scrolling on social media, put your phone down or walk away from your laptop. At the very least, close your browser. Taking a break from social media can curb your tendency to compare yourself to others by a lot! When you are on social media, remind yourself that the things you see on there, be they stuff that your friends share or photos that influencers upload, aren't ever the full picture. We all have our insecurities, after all. We all have our own unique problems and troubles. But odds are, none of us will ever upload them on Instagram for the world to see. I mean, would you? Of course, you wouldn't. So, remind yourself of that simple fact the next time you find yourself making comparisons. Then close your eyes, take a deep breath, and tell yourself that you are good enough as you are. Because that, my friend, is the honest truth.

CHAPTER 2
YOUR BODY LANGUAGE

What? I didn't even say anything!

When you think about communicating with others, your mind likely goes directly to *talking*. But in reality, you can communicate more with your body language than your words. So before we get into what to say, let's talk about how you say it. Your posture, your gestures, your mimics... Like it or not, they all communicate something about you. They all give some sort of impression to the people you're talking to, either positive or negative.

Communicating using your body language is known as non-verbal communication. For instance, smiling when you meet someone for the first time implies that you're happy to meet them *before* you even have the chance to say the words, "It's nice to meet you." But if it's a fake-looking smile on your face while saying, "It's nice to meet you," the person will get the message that you'd rather be somewhere else. Crossing your arms in front of yourself when you meet someone new is also a form of non-verbal communication. This one gives off negative signals, though. It essentially closes you off from the person before you. If you were a building, your crossed arms would be a closed gate, barring entry, leaving people on the outside.

You can use non-verbal communication to convey

a host of different things. How you feel now, what you think about someone or a situation, or how people should approach you. Don't let this overwhelm you, as if this is yet another category of things working against you. Once you understand the different types of non-verbal communication and the effects they have, you can use them to your advantage, and your conversations will be much more effective. When you give appropriate non-verbal cues, not only do you eliminate a negative impression, but you actually produce a positive impression. You may start out just wanting not to feel awkward, but you can go further with these tools and actually cause others to feel appreciated and want to connect with you more. Some key types of non-verbal communication are:

- body language
- movement
- posture
- gestures
- space
- paralanguage
- facial expressions
- eye contact
- touch

That's quite a bit to remember, isn't it? Luckily, they're all fairly easy to understand. Take *body language*, for instance. This is simply how you position your body when interacting with others. Holding one arm with your opposite hand can signal that you're nervous and worried about your appearance, not comfortable enough to let your hands hang or move freely.

Next up is *movement*. This is related to body language, but it's not quite the same. Movement refers to how you move your arms, legs, and body. Picking up speed when you see someone you don't want to talk to coming up to you is an example of movement. So are sitting, fidgeting, and being stiff. Letting your eyes wander when someone's speaking to you, for instance, will easily say— nay scream— "I'm so bored!" regardless of how many "uh-huh"s you offer. However, sitting still and letting your eyes move from the speaker's eyes to the hand gestures they're making and then back again is a movement that gives the "I'm present, interested, and paying attention" message to the one who's speaking.

Then there's your *posture*. The way you stand or sit in a given space can be very telling. If you're sitting with your back ramrod straight, you can signify you're alert, awake, and paying attention. If you're slouching and hunching forward, on the other hand, that can suggest you're tired or frustrated. It can also show that you're spending way too much time hunched over a computer screen, and if that's the case, that might be something you want to get looked at.

Not to be confused with movement, *Gestures* are in a category of their own. Using energetic, animated hand gestures when describing something definitely falls into this category. So is giving someone a thumbs up or making a goofy face.

Space refers to how much space you put between yourself and others. This can carry pretty subtle and obvious meanings. For instance, if you have a crush on the classmate sitting to your left, you might find yourself leaning to the left as you take notes in class. Why? Because in doing so, you eliminate some of the space between you and try to get closer to them. Similarly, if you dislike someone, you might take a step back as they're talking to you, literally putting some space between them. Generally speaking, you want to give enough space between you and another person that both of you still have a "personal bubble," but not so much space that they have to speak louder for you to hear them. If you're standing more than a full step away from a person, they will likely feel like you want to slip away and are looking for a brief, surface-level conversation.

Paralanguage refers to things like the tone and pitch of your voice, its volume and intonations—that is to say, which words you emphasize and how. You can convey sarcasm or sincerity with your emphasis. If you're going to go on a trip to an amusement park, you might raise the volume and pitch of your voice as you talk about it. This would make clear just how excited you are about the trip. But if you're trying to console a friend who is grieving, your tone should naturally become slower, quieter, and warmer.

Facial expressions should need little to no explanation. I'm sure you are familiar by now with what things like smiling mean. You may even recall that expression your mother would get when you were in trouble as a kid, but she can't yell at you in public. That look screams, "You're in trouble once we get home." You may have had some trouble meeting your mom's eye when she got that expression. Not being able to meet someone's eye can give them the "I'm afraid" or "I'm ashamed" messages. Sometimes it may also mean you don't respect the person standing before you.

Finally, there's *touch*. Resting your hand briefly on someone's shoulder, patting them on the back, squeezing their hand... These are all things that can convey love, friendship, or affection through the sense of touch alone. Such things can also communicate support. Think back. When was the last time you got a really good hug? How did that make you feel? Did you doubt for a moment that the person embracing you truly cared for you? That right there is the power of touch.

ATTITUDE AND GESTURES

When you see someone, what part of their body do you look at first? Vanessa Van Edwards asked this question to her audience the day she gave her TED talk about body language. The talk, which has since gone viral, points out that we actually look at someone's hands before we even look at their faces when we first meet them (Van Edwards, 2017). This is because our hands communicate our intentions. The more hand gestures we use while we talk, the more we underline and emphasize what we're trying to say. The more we do that, the more confident we appear.

Imagine that you have two professors. One is very animated. She uses her hands a lot when describing wars, battles, and treaties—she's a history professor, let's say. She clearly likes her job and gets very excited about all the things that she's teaching. You would probably like attending her classes and feel more engaged in her lessons. Now, let's say there's another history professor in class. Sometimes he substitutes for your original professor. He seldom ever uses his hands to describe things. In fact, he mostly keeps them clasped behind his back as he goes over dates and figures. Now tell me, which class sounds more engaging to you? Which would be more likely to draw you in? Which would cause you to remember more of what was said?

The answer, in this case, is obvious. But why should you like the first professor's lessons? The short answer? It's because human emotions are contagious. The history professor you like is clearly excited about her job. She has no trouble showing this excitement, as reflected in hand gestures. You can sense the excitement she has by watching her body language and gestures. You, in fact, catch her excitement by watching those very same things.

This isn't just true of hand gestures and body language. It's also true of expressions. Imagine that you're walking down the street, and you see a friend coming toward you. Your friend is rushing somewhere, so she doesn't have time to stop. But she is genuinely happy to see you and gives you a big smile. You return her smile, suddenly feeling lighter, happier. Why? Because you caught her happiness. If your friend had looked afraid as she was walking towards you, you similarly would have caught her fear. This logic applies to all emotions we feel as they reflect on our body language, expressions, and gestures. However, knowing that emotions and attitudes are important doesn't necessarily make them easy to convey. There's an element of vulnerability that you'll have to make a decision about beforehand; otherwise, you'll likely try to protect yourself by stiffening up and not revealing any emotion at all. It may feel safer that way at the moment, but it works against you. By stifling your enthusiasm about seeing an old friend, the friend doesn't think, *Aww, he's excited to see me, but he's too afraid to show it.* Rather, he thinks, *Wow, he's not glad to see me at all. I wonder what I did to him?* Now he's uncomfortable, you're uncomfortable, and it's all off to a bad start. However, by choosing to make yourself vulnerable and showing the emotion that you feel, whether it makes you look foolish or not, you send a clear message to others about what you're feeling, and it puts them at ease. That is by far the better foundation to build on.

Let's go back to the cafeteria scenario. Imagine you're that poor, nervous kid again, wanting to meet new friends. As you introduce yourself, your nervousness reflects on your expression, body language, hand gestures, posture, and paralanguage. In short, it infuses every aspect of non-verbal communication. As you approach the kids at the table, you give them the "I'm nervous" signal loud and clear. The kids in question pick up on this signal. Without knowing why, the whole group is now a little tense. As a result, your chat with the group is a bit awkward at best. But the thing is, it doesn't have to be. You have the power to control what kind of attitude you convey to the people you interact with. This means you can be conscious of the signals you're sending to others by being conscious of your non-verbal signals. Not only to avoid making people feel uncomfortable but to actually take things in the other direction and make them feel positive.

Take a look at a positive scenario. You've just been called into an interview for an internship you really want to get. You're a little nervous, but you did all your research and prepared well for the interview. You're ready. The non-verbal message you want to convey to your interviewer is that you're ready and you're confident. You can do that by being very conscious of your non-verbal signals. For instance, you're waiting for your interviewer in the lobby or the waiting room of an office. When your interviewer walks in, you get up to your feet and shake their hand firmly, with confidence. You smile when you see them, making sure that that smile reaches your eyes. You keep smiling—naturally, not forcefully— throughout your interview. As you sit down in the interviewer's room, you're very conscious of your posture and how you are sitting. A great way to convey confidence at this moment is to sit with your back straight and chin up. You can also plant both your feet firmly on the ground and place your hands on top of one another to signal that you're friendly and open. You can emphasize these points even further by being conscious of your tone. You can opt for a friendly, confident tone that isn't too loud. In doing all this, you would be giving all the right messages to your interviewer and setting the right tone. In other words, you'd be ensuring that your interviewers caught the right emotion and mood from you, making it much more likely that you'd get the job.

CONVERSATIONAL BODY LANGUAGE

So, if we're giving all these different signals, what kinds of messages are you sending when talking to others? What is your body language communicating when you're meeting someone new? Is it saying that you're nervous? That you don't actually want to talk to them? That you're closed off or tense? Or is it saying that you're happy to meet them? That you're comfortable? That you'd like to get to know them more?

Let's say that your body language is giving off signals that you don't actually want to be giving, like that you'd rather cut the conversation short and move on. How can you change that? How can you use your body language to say, "I'm confident, and I'd like to talk to you," or "I'm very comfortable with this conversation and want to keep getting to know you."? You can do several things to give these messages or similar ones. If you ever worry that someone's not enjoying your company, you can also watch their body language for these signs. By doing so, you can quell those self-conscious worries that might be popping up in your mind, wondering, *What if they don't like me?*

- **Lean in:** This is an easily observable sign. Let's say you're sitting at a table directly across from someone, and they're telling you a story. How can you make clear that you're very interested in it without continually interrupting them to say, "Ooh, how interesting"? By leaning towards them, even if it's just a little. Leaning in toward someone literally closes the distance between the two of you, and it also gives a feeling of doing so emotionally. It shows that you are focusing on the person intentionally and, as a result, leaning *away from* other distractions. The same technique also works in group settings, such as meetings or lectures. If you lean in slightly, you may notice the speaker catching your gaze as they notice that you have given them more noticeable focus than the rest of their audience.

- **Touch someone's arm:** Touching someone's arm briefly while talking to them can be very communicative. Touch, as we know, conveys love, friendship, and even trust. If a friend is telling you how they've been having a rough time of late, touching their arm and giving a quick squeeze can say, "I'm sorry that you're going through this, but I'm here for you." Touching a date's arm or hand quickly while walking or sitting at a cafe can tell them that you really like them without having to utter a word.

- **Don't press your lips together:** When we're nervous, we tend to press our lips rather tightly together. This all but screams, "I'm very tense right now." It's understandable that you're nervous when you're meeting someone new. But remember that the feelings our emotions communicate are contagious. So, take a deep breath and relax your lips when you notice you're pressing them together.

- **No turtlenecks:** I don't mean the shirt style; feel free to wear those if that's your thing. The turtle neck I'm referring to is when you keep your shoulders high toward your ears as if you're mid-shrug. It shows that you're either embarrassed— and, therefore, trying to hide in your shell like a turtle—or that you lack confidence. So, try to lower your shoulders when you catch yourself doing this and stand up straight if you can. A quick posture-correcting trick is to lean back into a relaxed stance and move your ears back over your shoulders as if trying to eavesdrop on someone behind you.

- **Watch where you point your feet:** Let's imagine you're on your feet, conversing with someone you don't know too well— like a classmate you've seen around but haven't talked to before. Look down very quickly. Where are your feet pointing? Are they pointing toward the door? If so, you're sending off the "I want this conversation to be over as quickly as possible so that I can bolt out of that door" message. In other words, you're communicating the fact that you're nervous. If you don't actually want to bolt out the door, adjust your stance so your feet are pointing toward the classmate you're talking to. This will tell them that you're interested in what they have to say and are giving them your full attention.

- **Go ahead and cross your legs:** Crossing your legs when you're sitting down communicates a very different message than crossing your arms. Crossing your arms says that you're closed off and don't want to talk. Crossing your legs, on the other hand, says that you're actually quite comfortable with the person you're talking to. Why? Because crossing your legs actually puts your body off balance, and it also takes longer to stand and leave. By adopting this stance, you're telling the person before you that you're settling in to talk and that you're comfortable being off balance or vulnerable with them. Let's say you're talking to a good friend and have leaned back and crossed your legs. Take a look at how your friend is sitting. Are they also crossing their legs? If so, you should know they're also very comfortable with you as well!

SOME TIPS FOR BEING MORE APPROACHABLE AND FRIENDLY

Now that you know basic conversational body language, let's move on to approachability. If you're having trouble meeting and/or connecting with new people, you want to think carefully about this. Have you ever started scrolling on your phone to look busy instead of alone? You're trying to hide your vulnerability, but instead, you hide your interest in meeting people. All too often, people get themselves into a terrible cycle when they don't have anyone to talk to, so they preoccupy themselves with something else to avoid appearing awkward and ultimately close themselves off, which keeps anyone else from talking to them! I see this in my teenage daughter often. We recently moved, and she went to a local gathering of other teens in our area. I think she imagined that someone there would walk up to her with open arms and a warm greeting, strike up a dazzling conversation, and introduce her to the larger group. But she quickly discovered that the other teens weren't any more likely to start talking to someone new than she was, and the other kids all gravitated toward each other because they'd known each other a long time. So to keep from looking like a loner, standing in the corner by herself, my daughter sat down and started to draw. She's a great artist and always keeps a notebook with her. I think she secretly hoped it would be a conversation starter, and someone would walk by, see her drawings and stop to talk about them. It could have worked out that way if she made herself seem more approachable by looking up to smile at people who passed by or appeared interruptable in some way. But no, she sat hunched over her notebook, never making eye contact with anyone, effectively becoming part of the background. When I pointed this out to her, she seemed to understand, but it was just too hard for her to remain vulnerable and not have her "security notebook" to hide in. But the thing about hiding is when you hide, you're *hidden*. I know, genius, right? But you'll blend into the background if you don't *look* like you're available to talk to. To complicate things further, you not only want to look available and interested in talking but also friendly and unintimidating. Seeing as you can't just walk up to someone and say, "I come in peace," as though you were some alien creature from another world, you communicate all this through your body language. But how on earth do you do that?

For starters, pay attention to what kind of expression you're wearing. Are your lips pressed tightly together? Is your brow furrowed? Are you frowning? If you answered "yes," you might want to wipe that expression off your face. Because you might as well be wearing a big, blaring "do not approach" sign on your forehead, with flashing red lights and all. So, let's say that a classmate you don't know very well has approached you and introduced himself. Remove the "do not approach" sign. Relax your lips, unfurrow your brow, and try to smile if you can. It doesn't have to be a big, wide smile, but just a quick, small one to give your classmate the green light.

Next, make sure your body language is as open as possible. What does that mean? It means don't cross your arms. Remember how we linked crossed arms to closed gates? Well, open those gates! That's the only way you can start letting people in. And remember what we said about watching where you point your feet? Well, that actually applies to your whole body. Watch where you angle yourself. If someone's talking to you and you're angled away from them, you're saying, "I want to go." That's not very productive for keeping a conversation going, is it? Now, let's say that you're at a get-together or party where you don't know a lot of people. You'd like to start mingling, though. As you scan the room, you're bound to meet someone's gaze at some point. If and when that happens, give them a friendly smile. The effectiveness of a good smile can never be over-stated! However, you *do not* want to just quickly look away. That would give the impression you're watching them from afar. Instead, give a smile, and continue scanning the room. You then have the *option* to say something to the person you made eye contact with if you'd like, or they may approach you, but the important thing is that you've left the option open without an obligation. When you're at a party or among a crowd of some sort, try to keep from looking down at the ground. I mean, how can you meet anyone new if you don't give yourself a chance to meet their gaze or catch someone's eye?

Everyone has their own habits and quirks. So, while these are the general tricks of the trade to become more approachable, you might have some habits making you appear less approachable than you want to be. So what's the best way to overcome these habits? Ask a trusted friend how your body language comes across. People who spend a lot of time with you and care about you might notice things about how you sit, stand, or even walk that you might have never considered.

Having read all this, you might think this is a bit much. I mean, does body language really matter all that much? Do you have to remember and pay attention to all of this? The short (and probably annoying) answer is yes, you do. Like it or not, we all judge people and assume things about them based on their body language alone. Yes, you do as well, whether you realize it or not. The judgments we make about others based on their body language can have really big consequences, at least according to social scientists Amy Cuddy. They can affect whom we hire for a job position or whom we ask to the prom (Cuddy, 2012). So, think carefully about what your body language says about you when you're meeting new people. It may well lead you down one path over another.

Build a Conversation

without it falling apart

CHAPTER 3
STARTING A CONVERSATION

stands in corner, pretending to be interested in the wall decor

You've mastered the art of body language. Now, you need to master the art of starting a conversation as well—you know, with actual words. If you want to make friends, build relationships, and get to know people, you need to start talking to strangers. Shocking, I know! But only through talking and conversation can you turn strangers into acquaintances, acquaintances into friends, and friends into close friends and loved ones. The first step to achieving all of this is starting an actual conversation. What if you walk up to someone, open your mouth, and nothing comes out? Well, the odds are that's going to be a fairly awkward situation now, isn't it? With that said, let us begin!

HOW TO TALK TO STRANGERS

So, you're in an environment where you don't know anyone. Maybe you're at a business convention. Maybe you just started a new job, or there's a block party in your new neighborhood. You're surrounded by people, but they're all strangers to you. You're trying to work up the nerve to go up to talk to one of them. But when you walk up, what will you say? How do you get them to talk to you, rather than saying "hey" and standing with you in awkward silence, then walking away?

Before we move on, let's briefly review your approach. You've spotted someone in the crowd, and you'd like to go up to them and introduce yourself. First, you need to double-check your body language. So you stand up straight with your arms falling confidently at your side, keeping them visible. You walk up to your mark with a smile, or at least a neutral expression, rather than a frozen one. You're giving multiple non-verbal signals that you are a great person to talk to. Got that? Good! Now onto the next step...

When you initiate a conversation with a stranger, any stranger, you need an opener, or your opening line. You might be stressing quite a bit about this. You might be thinking, "What do I even say?" The reality is your opener doesn't need to be complicated, and it doesn't need to wow and amaze. In fact, if it did, it might catch the person off guard instead of making them feel comfortable and at ease. You might be surprised to know that the simplest opener is often the best one to go with. So, when in doubt, just go with, "Hey, how are you?" (Hailey, 2022). You can also reference something around you, perhaps something that you both just saw, like a presentation or a performance. "Hi, that was pretty interesting, wasn't it? Have you ever seen something like that before?" would be a very natural way to start a discussion about a shared experience. Here are a few other conversation-starter ideas you can have in your arsenal:

- Seen anything interesting lately?
- Do you enjoy events like these?
- I've never been here before, have you?
- Maybe you could suggest something to eat/do.

Once you've walked up to someone and initiated a conversation, you have done the hardest part. Next up is the handshake. You might not like handshakes, but it's a good idea to work one in if you can. This is because handshakes communicate a lot of information about you through the sense of touch—something that plays a huge role in body language, if you recall. Interestingly enough, handshakes also trigger the release of certain chemicals in your body (and the body of the person you're talking to) that allow you to bond and make any interaction feel more personal (Hailey, 2022). How cool is that!

A good handshake, then, can be essential for starting up a worthwhile conversation. You can extend your hand either during your opener or immediately after it. Ever wondered if your handshake is a good one? Well, let's evaluate, shall we:

- Are your hands dry?
- Is your handshake firm?
- Did you maintain eye contact?

If you answered these questions with a "yes," congratulations, you have a good handshake! You probably have no trouble understanding why keeping your hands dry is important for a good handshake. But why must a handshake be firm? Because a "firm" handshake signals to the other person that you're confident and capable. It's something that interviewers often pay attention to when they're meeting with you for a potential job or internship, for instance. Of course, balance is key where "firmness" is concerned. You don't want to squeeze the other person's hand too tightly like you're trying to hurt or dominate them. And eye contact shows you respect the other person and want to be engaged in this conversation. Looking down or away while shaking someone's hand could communicate timidity, disrespect, or disinterest in the person or conversation.

As you start to engage with the person, consider

these tips to help you approach someone and start to chat without coming across as awkward.

- If you have difficulty meeting people's eyes, remember that holding eye contact for only about three to five seconds is enough to let people know you're interested in what they're saying. Feel free to then look at something nearby, look at what the other person is looking at or talking about, but then come back to meet their eyes *periodically*, not constantly.
- If the thought of smiling at a stranger makes you think you'll have a goofy look on your face, just think to yourself, 'Today is a great day.' The expression that naturally graces your face as you think of a beautiful day or a nice memory is the kind of expression you want here. This will make smiling easier and more genuine, which is exactly what you want to be.
- If you're unsure when you should tell someone your name in conversation, ask for theirs first. Then you'll be expected to give yours anyway.
- If you've been talking to someone for a bit and don't know what their name is, don't

convince yourself that you should have known by now, so now you have to "play it off." That is *never* the case. Instead, simply say something like, "By the way, what was your name?" Then go ahead and introduce yourself. Even if you forget their name later on, ask them before you end the conversation, "Tell me your name again?" You can laugh about your poor memory, but it's always better to ask again than pretend you know.

STARTING A CONVERSATION

So, you've introduced yourself to someone you don't know. They've introduced themselves back, and you've each found out how the other is doing. That's great. *But what now?*

The short answer is, you ask questions. You want to draw out the other person so they get talking. We'll look at a lot of suggestions of questions you can ask, but keep in mind that many of them will need some sort of preface, or they'll seem out of the blue and odd. You can start with a phrase like these before you ask your question:

- I was just wondering…

- The other day, someone asked me this, and I want to see what you think...

If you're having trouble coming up with things to say or questions to ask, take a page out of comedian Jerry Seinfeld's book. When Seinfeld is talking to people he doesn't know, he always asks them numbers-based questions. These are easy-to-answer questions with definite answers. Let's say you're at a party, and you've met someone. You can ask, "So, when did you get here?" The person you're talking to will be able to readily answer this question without any awkwardness—assuming they're not the host, in which case, don't, you know they live there. Other examples of number-based questions you could ask might be:

- How long have you known the host?
- How many of these conferences have you been to?
- How long will you be here?

If you're more introverted, starting conversations off with such questions might be perfect for you (Van Edwards, 2016). Why? Because introverts actually use fewer words during the day than extroverts! If you're an introvert, this is because you like to think and observe before you jump into a conversation. Asking numbers-based questions allows you to do that while asking good questions that can keep conversations going. Say, for example, that you met someone at a party who told you they switched careers in recent years. How might this conversation go if you ask numbers-based questions? Well, let's see:

You: "Oh, when did you switch jobs?"

Them: "About three years ago."

You: "Wow. So what did you do before?"

As it plays out here, the conversation can give you a very good jumping-off point to get to know this person better. For instance, the rest of the conversation might go as follows:

You: "That must have been very difficult for you. Did you know anyone in the field?"

Them: "I didn't know anyone, but everyone else was already well networked. So, I had a bit of a tough time at first."

If number questions aren't for you, you can always turn to tried and tested conversation starters. Asking "How are you?" is a classic for a reason. But so is noticing something about the person you're talking to and asking a question about it. People love talking about themselves, especially if it involves something they were hoping others would notice. If they start talking more, it takes a great deal of pressure off of you. So if you can notice something unique about them— clothing, jewelry, hairstyle...— go for it.

Say you saw that someone is wearing a unique necklace. You could ask about it, and the conversation might go like this:

You: "I really like your necklace. Where did you get it?"

Them: "Oh, thank you. It was actually my mother's. She got it when she was my age."

You: "Oh wow, that's even more special. I love her style! I have a couple of things from my mom too, and they're my favorite things to wear. Don't you love the quality of vintage things?"

Let's say you're at a dinner gathering, and you don't know the people sitting next to you. What do you do? You start by asking one or two of the following questions and see where the conversation goes from there:

- Have you tried the [insert dish name here]?
- What's your favorite food / cuisine?
- What's the weirdest thing you've ever eaten?
- I've tried making this before, but it didn't turn out this well. Do you like to cook?

Moving on, we'll take a look at school settings. Say that you've been assigned a group project and don't know any of the people in your group. Here are some questions you can ask to get to know them before tackling the work you need to do:

- Have any of you met before?
- How do you feel you're doing in the class?
- What do you guys usually do after class?
- Have you watched the new [insert movie title] movie yet?

That's all well and great, but what if you have a friend and you haven't been able to catch up in a while? How do you restart the conversation? How do you bridge the gap? Alternatively, let's say you've made a friend but don't know them very well yet. How can you get to know them? In both cases, you could start by asking some questions such as:

- It's been a while since we were able to talk. What's changed since I saw you last?
- Have you worked on anything exciting lately?
- What's something you're into these days?
- Do you ever think about what you'd like to do after you're finished with school?

- How's it going with [mention something you have discussed before]?

These are just some ideas for conversation starters. You can just as easily come up with your own. The trick to being able to do so is knowing *how* to ask effective questions. This means asking questions that prompt conversation rather than ones that can be answered with just a "yes" or "no." This is why asking what people think about [insert situation, book, movie, hobby, etc.] always works. They enable you to discover people's likes, dislikes, or thoughts and share your own.

One thing you should remember when coming up with conversation starters and questions is that you don't need to try to come up with something clever. You don't need to ask something really deep or meaningful. So, remember that and take some of the pressure off of yourself. The best conversation starters are simple ones.

YOU'RE IN A CONVERSATION! NOW WHAT?

As the back-and-forth of asking and answering questions begins to happen on both sides, you simply need to continue. You'll ask follow-up questions, and give your own insights. But somewhere around this point, it's possible that you could start to overthink the situation, and anxiety could set in, threatening to throw you off course. Right now, and as many times as is necessary, you'll need to **re-engage**.

Anytime you start to find yourself in a self-monitoring mode, where you're focusing too much on your own behavior and responses, you'll need to reset. I know, I know— this whole book is about being aware of your behavior, and now I'm saying not to pay attention to it? Well, not exactly. Right now, you're in the preparation phase, where it's important to think through a lot of details and possibilities. But when the time comes that you're in a conversation with someone, you'll need to find a balance between self-awareness and self-monitoring. When you're *self-aware*, you correct your posture and remind yourself to ask more questions while giving the speaker your attention. When you're *self-monitoring*, you don't even hear the words someone else is saying because you're consumed with your own voice in your own head. *Stop fidgeting. Don't look over there. Look interested. No, not like that. That probably makes me look dumb.* Meanwhile, you've missed what's going on because you're focused on yourself without allowing yourself to react naturally to the situation. To re-engage means to take a moment to breathe and remind yourself of why you're here. Whether it's to build a relationship or to learn from someone in school or business, at this moment, you are here to engage with this person. You're not going to ask the right questions because you've memorized this book like a script, but because you've tuned in to the person you're talking with, and certain questions and responses will come naturally, if you're paying attention. Refocus on the person in front of you and what they're trying to communicate to you. If they say something that's unclear, don't wonder how it will make you look to ask a clarifying question, *just ask the question*. Because it's not about how it makes you look but how you can understand them better. Once you make that switch in your focus, you'll be able to be more present, and the rest will come more easily.

Say that someone you met told you that they didn't like that new Marvel movie. A good question you can ask in this case is, "Oh, why is that?" This way, you can keep the dialogue going and find out a bit more about this person's tastes and thoughts.

Asking questions is good, but communication is a two-way street. If you don't add in commentary about your own life or perspective occasionally, and only rapid-fire questions directed to the other person, they will start to feel like they're in an interview— or worse yet, an interrogation! You should also be sharing some information about yourself in between questions, which creates the back-and-forth movement of conversation that keeps it from falling flat. Plus, if the person you're talking with is a good conversationalist as well, they will likely be throwing some questions in your direction also. For instance, they may ask you, "What about you? Did you like that new Marvel movie," with "Actually, I did/didn't like it because..." Alternatively, once the person you're talking to tells you why they didn't like the movie, you can jump in with, "That's interesting. I really liked/disliked it myself because..." If you're still unsure about when you should share information about yourself, here's a helpful formula you can follow:

1. Start by asking a question.
2. Ask a follow-up question once you've received an answer.
3. Share a bit of information about yourself related to what has just been discussed.
4. *repeat*

How about online conversations? We live in the age of social media, where a lot of conversation takes place on Instagram, Twitter, Facebook, and even various dating apps. On the one hand, the conversation can be easier online as you have more time to think about what you're saying. On the other, it can be quite difficult because a lot of things can be lost in translation, so to speak, when you're communicating in writing. Sarcasm, for instance, might not come through clearly. Irony will almost always fail. Given this obstacle, there are a couple of rules you should keep in mind when talking to others online:

1. Know why you're reaching out to a complete stranger online. In other words, have a clear reason to do so. "I saw a picture of your cat on Insta, and she's really cute. I wondered if you know her breed?" could be a good opening line that immediately communicates why you're talking to that person. So is, "My friend [insert friend's name] told me you'll be part of our group project, so I wanted to introduce myself. Have you worked with this group before?" Both these options are better than sending a message that just says "Hey!" which will probably leave the person you're talking to wondering, "Why on earth is this stranger reaching out to me?"

2. If you already know the person you're talking to online or have talked with them online/in person before, reference something you've already talked about before. "I remembered that you said awhile back that you liked reading classic mysteries. I saw a bookstore that was having a sale on them and thought you might be interested" is an example of this. So is "How did that business meeting go? I remember you were a bit nervous about it."

3. Ask to meet up in person once you know someone well enough. Online conversations can be convenient, but nothing beats face-to-face conversation. Not sure how to ask someone to meet up? If you have a mutual interest, you can always propose doing something related to it. For instance, if you're both into basketball and there's a basketball game coming up, you can ask your friend if they'd like to go. You can also just invite the person with whom you're speaking to a group meet-up that's already taking place, thus making them feel included.

CHAPTER 4
FILLING A CONVERSATION

I've got this. I'm hilarious.

Using humor... and NOT being
offensive... pg. 68

Me? Offensive? How?

Asking questions... and NOT being
annoying... pg. 72

Well, I know all about that already.

Using your knowledge...and NOT
being obnoxious... pg. 76

Sorry, I zoned out. What?

Giving your attention... and NOT
being fake... pg. 83

S tarting a conversation with someone you've only just met is hard. For some people, though, the real challenge might be keeping the conversation going. Once you've successfully managed to start a conversation, the pressure is on. You feel as if you must keep the person you're talking to engaged. You must be interesting. You must be funny. You must put the person you're talking to at ease so that they'll be more open to talking. Those are so many things to consider, so many balls in the air. It's more than understandable why you might drop one or two such balls while you're juggling frantically. So how can you keep from juggling in this panic-frenzied way? What can you do to keep a conversation going with ease and without stressing over details? Many, many things.

First off, realize that the fate of the conversation really isn't resting on your shoulders alone. There is at least one other person involved, and they have things to contribute and questions to ask as well. Re-engage if necessary, and try to relax your mind to enjoy the conversation. As you do so, you can try out one or all of the four tools in this chapter to boost any conversation and make it a memorable one. The tools are humor, questions, knowledge, and attention. But before we get into those topics, here is a simple, yet game-changing tip to avoid lags in conversation before they begin. It is to **end your statements with a downward tone**. By that, I'm referring to the actual pitch of your voice. If you were to say the word, "me" to someone, imagine the difference in meaning whether your voice slides up or down at the end. "Me." vs. "Me?" Go ahead and try it out loud. In most English-speaking countries, but especially in America, a downward tone at the end of a sentence indicates that it is 1) finished, and 2) not a question. Obvious, I know. But chances are, you've made this mistake before, and it has caused you to "trail off," as you grasp for more things to fill the space of what *could have* been the end of your sentence. Not sure how? Then say, "me" one more time, but this time, hold your pitch steady, not sliding up *or* down. Go ahead, I'll wait. It may even sound like you're singing the word as you hold the tone saying, "meeee."

The impression this gives is that you're in the middle of a sentence, and there is more to come; so you can see the tension it could cause for both you and the listener if you do this at the *end* of a sentence. The listener becomes expectant for what's next, and you mentally panic, trying frantically to come up with an ending to the sentence. Often, you might go with, "... or something," or "...errr, whatever," because you don't actually have more to say, you're just grasping for filler words.

You can practice this concept with any number of statements. Say these sentences aloud, but hold a constant tone on the last word of each one.

"I've never been there before..."

"I'm an only child..."

"I can have that done by Friday..."

Imagine the uneasiness it would cause for you and the listener, as you try to find somewhere for your words to land, and they try to figure out what else you are trying to say.

Instead, if you simply end each of the same statements with a downward tone, you will achieve three benefits. First, you exude more confidence. Secondly, you give the other person a clear signal that it's their turn to speak and they have the opportunity to ask follow-up questions or continue in some other way. You also relax your brain a little, because you're not scrambling for an ending. This is of more value than you may realize. When your mind is calm, you'll be able to continue the conversation more freely. If someone asked you what you did over the weekend, and you answered that you went to the movies, you could have an easy, natural conversation that sounds something like this:

"What did you do last weekend?"

"I went to see a movie."

"Oh yeah? What did you see?"

"I saw the new superhero movie."

"Did you like it?"

"Yeah, I thought it was better than the last one."

If each of your sentences ends with a tone that clearly indicates you're finished with the sentence, the other person can speak, and the back-and-forth flows freely. You may be wondering if ending your sentences in this way might make you sound "short" with people. But as long as you still appear interested in the conversation (with your eye contact, open body language, warm tone, etc.), you won't give off that impression. But if instead, you end your first response in an upward or straight tone, you'll feel as if you have to keep adding words to your sentence. You can say all the same things, but in a more awkward way, that leaves the other person with nothing else to say afterward.

"What did you do last weekend?"

"I went to the movies— that new superhero movie— it was pretty good— I liked it better than the last one."

As you make a habit of ending your sentences more confidently, you'll find that it prevents a lot of awkwardness in conversation before it begins.

USING HUMOR (AND NOT BEING OFFENSIVE)

A proper joke can be a godsend at the right time. Is the conversation stalling? Don't worry; you can get things going again and lift everyone's mood in the process by throwing in a little joke. Is there a slight, awkward silence? Get them laughing and break the ice. Humor can be an easy way out. It can help to diffuse embarrassing situations and even manage your stress and anxiety. But "easy" isn't always good. Humor can be tricky because some jokes can easily offend people if you're not careful. It can cut off communication in a way that we don't want. It can put up a wall between you and others, preventing them from sharing things with you. How do you navigate this problem? How can you keep the mood light and enjoyable without upsetting anyone?

Have you ever heard the saying, "Read the room"? Well, using humor correctly requires having the ability to read the room. If you're old enough to read this, you probably know by now that making fun of another person to get a laugh offends them. Or when you're attending a somber event, making jokes would be viewed as disrespectful. These are obvious times when humor is out of line.

A more subtle problem is that humor can hurt

you and your relationships if you use it to avoid problems. If your significant other is talking to you about relationship troubles you've been having of late and you keep derailing the conversation by making light of things, then they will feel like they're not being heard and become frustrated and upset. Do this long enough, and it'll erode your relationship.

If a friend is having a vulnerable moment with you, what they're looking for isn't a way to avoid it. That's really what humor does in a serious situation — it diverts attention away from the matter at hand. For many of us, that's why we use it. Something uncomfortable comes up, and we want so badly to take the easy way out, get a laugh, and forget all about that sensitive subject. But ask yourself why the person brought up the uncomfortable topic in the first place. It wasn't because they wanted someone to make light of it or divert attention to something else. It's for you to listen to them and support them. If they open themselves up, only to find out that opening up isn't safe to do around you, you will effectively limit the depth of your relationship with that person, then and there. Instead, you need to restrain the humor for the time being, and support the one who's speaking. That doesn't even have to mean knowing what to say to them. You can even tell them exactly that; "I don't know what to say." Or perhaps ask them, "What do you need right now?" or "What can I do to help?" Being supportive really just means sitting quietly with them and listening, giving them the assurance that they have at least one person in the world who will do just that.

You might want to check your impulse to make jokes if you feel frustrated or nervous. If you disregard how nervous you feel on a date and try to diffuse the emotion by making a joke, you might be disregarding something that makes you feel uncomfortable. You might also be avoiding something that is a red flag. Or worse, you might end up offending your date, who is just as nervous as you are. I remember back to my high school days when I could not get the use of humor down. A group of us went out to eat before the homecoming dance. My date was a freshman, and this was her first high school dance. You can imagine how nervous she must have been. I was always a jokester, especially at the worst times. There was a point during the dinner before the meal came out when the group conversation had just died. In the uneasy silence, some in the group were looking at my date when she said, "Why is everyone looking at me?" Now, there are so many things I could have said at that moment, but the awkward jokester version of me came out when I said, "Because you're so funny looking." That's when she excused herself, and the other girls joined her in the bathroom. The young men at the table just smiled, knowing their dates were suddenly going much better. I'm sure you would be shocked to find out that she didn't say two words to me the rest of the evening.

Similarly, making a joke might not be the best idea if you feel frustrated with people. Take a group project, for example. The frustration you feel might be pointing to communication errors within the group that can prevent you from finishing the project well. Try to pay greater attention to such feelings when you have them so they can be dealt with, not just laughed off.

So how do you use humor correctly? Rule number one in this regard is to not put so much pressure on yourself. When we try to be deliberately funny, we often miss the mark because we try too hard, and it's unnatural. Think back to a time when you were truly funny. You probably were very relaxed at that moment, and the humor of the situation arose candidly. Think of the people you're funniest with. You are probably very comfortable around them, are you not?

All this means is that humor can be a great tool in your conversational kit, but only if it's natural, not forced, and restrained when necessary. The trick to using it at such times is to read the room and pay attention to your feelings and the feelings of others.

ASKING QUESTIONS (AND NOT BEING ANNOYING)

Asking questions can make anyone a little nervous, especially if you're talking to someone you only recently met. You might worry about coming across as a little irritating if you ask too many questions, like that kid who counters every response he's given with the question "Why?" except aged up. You might also worry that you're being a bit too invasive with your questions, like you're trying to pry or are invading someone's privacy. While having such worries is understandable, take a deep breath. The truth is, you're not being irritating or invasive. You're simply trying to better get to know the person you're talking to. The only way to do that is through questions and listening to what they have to tell you.

With that being said, the question is… What kinds of things should you ask? How do you ask questions effectively and actually manage to get to know the people you're talking to? How can you know if you're asking questions that will keep them talking? Or, if you are asking questions, these just seem to be… well, duds?

Let's start with open and closed questions. Closed questions are questions that have short yes or no answers. This doesn't necessarily mean that closed questions are always duds, but they do only return very brief responses. "Are you hungry?" would be a good example of one. After all, you can only answer it in so many ways. The most you can say after someone asks if you're hungry is, "Yes, I am. How about you?" The person you're talking to will then indicate whether they're hungry or not, and then... Well, either you need to find a new question to ask, or they do; that is, if you want the conversation to keep going. Open questions are the complete opposite of that. They're inquiries that prompt longer answers and draw out information, and usually begin with "How," "What," or "Why." For instance, "How did the class presentation go?" would be an open question. So would "What happened at work today?" or "Why did you end your date so soon?"

As a general rule, asking open questions is better than asking closed questions when trying to keep a conversation flowing. This is because closed questions cut off further avenues of discussion. Open questions, on the other hand, are great for opening conversations up. For instance, if you ask someone, "Do you need any help?" You might be told, "Nah." But if you rephrase it to, "What else do you need to organize the party?" the friend will have to think about what is left, and that could lead to discussion.

This doesn't mean that asking closed questions is necessarily bad for conversations. They're great for making sure you've understood things correctly. You'll be doing just that when you ask, "So, we're meeting tomorrow at 3:30 p.m.?" But the key to closed questions is knowing when to use them. If you ask a closed question when the conversation is flowing, you might kill that conversation. If your friend is telling you all about their date and you cut off the anecdotes they're sharing by asking, "So it went well, then?" and leaving it at that, you might prevent her from telling you more. So, be mindful of when you're asking closed questions, and try to ask open questions if you want to keep a conversation going.

A dud question would be one that tells you nothing. You see someone waiting in line for a concert and you ask, "You going to the concert?" Well, yeah, how'd you guess? No new information was received here. Instead, you could say, "I'm excited to see this group, have you ever seen them in concert before?"

Questions can be very powerful conversational tools. They can get people to think about matters more deeply and have more intimate conversations, allowing for better understanding between people.

For that to happen, though, you must bear certain rules in mind, regardless of what questions you are asking. First, you must avoid stacking questions. What this means is that you must ask your questions one at a time rather than firing off one question after another in a single breath. Doing the latter makes things a little difficult for the person you're talking to. You potentially confuse them as they try to figure out which question they should answer first. In this case, once they've answered the question, they might forget the next one and the next. This could lead to some awkward pauses and to a lot of interjections that go, "I'm sorry, what was the question?" It can easily overwhelm them and cause them to shut down. So separate your questions with their answers, and also remember to give feedback in between as well, as discussed in the last chapter. Both of these techniques used together will allow you to ask a greater number of questions while still feeling natural.

The second rule you should remember is to keep your questions as succinct as you can. Long-winded questions are another way to confuse the person you're talking to. In trying to answer you, their minds might become a little jumbled, trying to understand what you're asking. If you feel like you need to give a lot of background information, be sure to restate the question at the end so it's clear what you are asking.

Rule number three is to keep asking open questions when and where you can. This is how you can keep the ball rolling and open up new conversational avenues where and when you can. As long as you keep that in mind, you can avoid those pesky, awkward silent moments from taking hold of conversations and get to know the people you're talking to much better.

USING YOUR KNOWLEDGE (AND NOT BEING OBNOXIOUS)

"Nobody likes a know-it-all," or so the saying goes. This is because know-it-alls often come across as obnoxious. They appear to be trying to show off to others, which can be very irritating. The funny thing is that most people who come across as know-it-alls aren't trying to flaunt their knowledge or anything like that. Often, they're excited to share something they have learned or discovered. But instead of communicating that enthusiasm, they come across as annoying, boring, or obnoxious. So, how do you avoid this pitfall? How can you use your knowledge without driving your listeners crazy?

The secret to this is simple: You need to practice

humility (Rubin, 2007). Nobody is telling you not to share things you know with them. Being humble takes restraint and maturity, but it is a very important, and very attractive quality. How can you practice humility, you ask? Well, let me count the ways:

- **Give genuine compliments.** It's natural to want to impress others, but what's truly attractive others is for them to feel that *they* have made a good impression. If you're working with others on a group project, you wouldn't want to put the others' ideas down while promoting your own ideas as the only ones worthwhile. But at the same time, you don't want to remain silent and let the value you bring to the group go unnoticed. Remember that you *do* add value, and it's always helpful to prompt discussion with others, even if your ideas aren't implemented. To find the balance, you'll want to encourage others to speak, be respectful when they do, and then speak up yourself. Compliment the others' input, and emphasize their strengths. You could say, "That's a great point, it seems like you've had a lot of experience in this area," before making your suggestion. Most people will offer you the same respect for your input that you've just shown to them, both out of consideration, and because you've put them at ease by not making it a competition for the best impression. When it comes to compliments, get as specific as possible. Instead of just telling someone that they're helpful, tell them what they did that helped you. Acknowledge other people's abilities, knowledge, capabilities, and character whenever possible.

- **Be teachable.** Remember how you're not the only person who knows a thing or two about one subject or another? Being teachable will open doors for you in life that few other things will. Everyone has times when they're unsure of a situation and feels like they don't know what they're doing. The problem is that many try to "fake it till you make it," and put on an air of knowing what you're doing. The result is often appearing arrogant while making mistakes. Probably not what you're going for. What will set you apart is that you're humble enough to admit when you don't have the answers and submit yourself to another's instructions. This is both refreshing and encouraging to the one(s) you seek out for help. So find someone with experience in the area of your interest, choose an appropriate time to talk, and ask them some questions. It's a great way to explore their pool of knowledge and also make them feel seen and heard. Others can be more open to hearing you speak if they feel like their voice is heard.

- **Admit your faults.** This follows the same reasoning as the previous point about being teachable, but this is in a more direct way because it usually happens when you're being confronted by someone else. Don't be afraid of saying that you don't know the answer, or even "I was wrong." You're human. There are bound to be times when you don't know or aren't very confident of something, and times when you realize you were completely wrong. At some point, you might have the unpleasant experience of realizing you were wrong about something mid-conversation, discussion, or argument. If and when such a day comes, take a deep breath and say, "You know, you're right. I was wrong." Likewise, admit something is your fault when you realize it is your fault. Trust me; you would be doing yourself, the people around you, and the relationships you have with them a world of favor. Usually, you'll find that once you admit your mistake, the situation is diffused— even if it was a heated argument— and the others involved switch out of defensive mode and actually start to come alongside you in the discussion.

- **Lift up others.** It's important to remember that humility is not putting yourself down; it's lifting others up even higher. Ask the people around you their thoughts on different things, and give credit where credit is due. Is someone being very quiet in your group project discussion? Ask them what their thoughts on the subject are. Ask them how they think they should proceed or what they think they should do. Is your professor giving you praise about something in your group project? Speak up and say, "Actually, that was [insert name]'s idea, and I agree that it's spot on!" Don't be fooled into thinking you'll miss out on making a good impression if you pass that credit on. On the contrary, you will make an even better impression on the professor, the person whose idea it was, and all those in earshot when you pass along the praise.

- **Laugh at yourself.** Don't be afraid to poke fun at yourself every once in a while. Not all the time in a self-deprecating way. (Remember that putting yourself down does not equal humility.) But every now and then, especially if you've made a mistake. Address it head-on, and just laugh it off. This is something that will make you exponentially more relatable, human, and approachable.

- **Be respectful.** When talking to and engaging with others, and especially when you disagree with them, give them the same respect you would hope to receive from them. Just because someone is of a different mind than you doesn't mean you can be rude or dismissive of them. You can have a different perspective from someone and still manage to be kind and polite to them.

Now, how about when you're actually sharing a bit of knowledge? How do you share what you know without appearing to be bragging? There are several ways you can go about doing this (Corcoran, 2014):

- If you're sharing a story about something you've achieved or succeeded at, be sure to express your gratitude for it. Let's say you got into your dream college. Congrats! This is, of course, a great bit of news that you should share with your friends. But what would your friends, who are likely anxiously waiting for their own college acceptance letters, respond better to? Are you going to say, "Well, yeah, of course I got in," or "I'm so grateful that I got in"?

- Be self-deprecating when appropriate: This doesn't mean being self-deprecating all of the time, but remember that poking fun at yourself can be a very good idea occasionally. It can easily do away with the impression that you're bragging. You don't need to be the hero in all of your stories.

- Be brief: Don't go on and on about your achievements and accomplishments. Your friends might be very happy you got into your dream college, but if that's all you can talk about for the next few hours, then odds are they'll be rolling their eyes at you sooner than anticipated. The same goes for something you are passionate about or an area of expertise.

- Make accomplishments and successes personal: Focusing on why that school was so important to you might be a better idea than that school being in the Ivy League if you're telling your friends about getting into your dream school.

GIVING YOUR ATTENTION (AND NOT BEING FAKE)

Conversation isn't just about talking. It's equal parts talking and listening, which work together to gain understanding. Listening skills are just as vital as speaking skills for building good relationships and creating understanding between you and others. Oftentimes, though, we only give the *appearance* that we're listening, because our mouths aren't moving. If you're constantly thinking of what you're going to say next in a conversation rather than what the person in front of you is saying, then trust me, you need to work on this area. Even if you know what the person is saying, you usually won't understand the significance of what they're saying. You won't pick up on the more subtle cues they're giving, nor understand just how much they care (or don't care) about what they're saying. If you're not truly listening to a friend when they're trying to talk to you about something, you're risking frustrating, hurting, or offending them. Do this for long enough, and your relationship with your friend can deteriorate. They might become distant from you, and understandably so. Why would anyone continue to bear their soul to someone who is clearly more interested in themself?

How do you become a good listener, then, and not just *look* like a good listener? How can you actively and attentively hear what you are being told? Here are three rules that show a person they have your attention:

Wait your turn. Don't interrupt people when they're speaking to you. This doesn't mean don't ask for clarification when you don't understand something. But if you're continually cutting in when someone else is speaking, the other person can become frustrated, irritated, and lose their train of thought. This can be tough if you never feel like you, yourself, are heard. Cutting in and interrupting almost becomes a survival mechanism, especially in groups. It's important to see how that comes across to others. If they are talking, it is better to let them talk over you than to offend them by interrupting and needing to be heard. If you're really having a hard time getting a chance to speak, try interjecting just briefly to let the group know you're waiting for a chance to speak. It could be something like, "I've got something to add to that when you're done, but keep going."

It's especially frustrating to be in the middle of a story or explanation when someone jumps in and sums up your story for you. Such as, "...when you made that decision—" "I know you were upset that I didn't tell you ahead of time." Not only could you be completely missing what they're trying to say, but even if your assumption is correct, people want to say all that they've prepared themselves to say. When you don't allow them to get it all out, they will walk away feeling unheard and undervalued. They could also feel the need to start over and try again because you didn't get the point the first time. So it doesn't really save time when you cut people off. Just don't do it.

If you have a difficult time breaking the habit of interrupting, try this trick. Physically lean back a bit in your chair or with your stance. (Just slightly, mind you. You don't want to give the impression you're trying to get away!) Normally, leaning in would be a good thing. We naturally want to lean in when we speak so it's easier to be heard, and it conveys that someone has our attention. But in this case of being tempted to interrupt, putting yourself in a physical position that makes it harder to be heard gives you an extra obstacle to cross before you speak.

Eye Contact. Let's say your boss is conducting a business meeting. Would he be more likely to think you're actively listening to him if your eyes are fixed on him or on the windows? Would he feel that you're focused on the information he is giving if you're leaning towards him and listening or if you're looking at the clock or scrolling on your phone? In which case do you think he'd be more likely to snap at you to pay attention? In which case would you be more likely to understand and remember all the information he's giving you?

Only give advice when it's wanted. Let's say that your friend is very upset and crying on your shoulder. Maybe literally, but at least figuratively. Maybe they had a huge fight with their significant other, or they've been feeling a lot of pressure at work and feel like they can't cope. Whatever the case may be, remember that sometimes people just need to unburden themselves. Your friend doesn't expect you to have solutions to all their problems. They don't expect you to wave a magic wand and fix things for them. They don't even expect you to know what to say. More often than not, all they expect is for you to listen to them and give them your undivided attention. They want you to lend them your ear so that they can talk about what they're going through and vent. It's important that you let them, without jumping in with advice and suggestions as to what they should do. If you don't, they will probably feel unable to say everything they need or want to say. If this happens often enough, they might clam up and stop turning to you when they need to talk. This will inevitably impact your relationship. But what if you're not sure whether or not they want advice? What if you can't tell if they want you just to listen or make suggestions instead? That's perfectly alright. If that is the case, wait until they've finished telling you the whole story without interrupting them. Need to ask clarifying questions? Ask them. Give your full focus and attention. When they're finished, ask them, "Do you want to know what I think?" They may tell you, "Sure," just out of politeness, but that still gives you a green light to share your thoughts. After you do, you'll get a sense of whether they want to keep discussing it or if they have already said everything they wanted to say. If you don't have any suggestions or advice to give them, then that's fine too. You can simply say that you're sorry they're going through a hard time, and they can always vent to you if they need to. Remind yourself that your friend only really needs you to be there for them, nothing more.

FILLING SILENCES

Before we wrap things up, there's one final tidbit you should be aware of. That is what to do when you run out of things to say. We'll talk about awkward silences more in the next section, but it's worth mentioning here as we talk about filling gaps in a conversation. We've all experienced that moment when you're talking to someone, and suddenly you have no idea what to say or how to keep the conversation going. You likely know the feeling of when an uncomfortable silence tries to take hold of the conversation. A situation like this can happen easily with strangers you're just meeting or with someone you're intimidated by. If it does, you might be tempted to find a new topic of conversation to latch onto. What you should consider doing instead is turning to a topic that will allow you to get to know them better. Let's say you're out on a first date. The awkward silence seems to creep in as you sit at a restaurant, painfully searching for something to say, and the waiter *could not be taking any longer* to bring your food. Use this moment to either get their opinion on something nearby: "Wow, interesting decor in this place, huh?" Or, turn to a shared experience, like that movie you just saw together. Ask about their favorite or least favorite scene. Alternatively, turn to shared interests. If they mentioned something before, like how they enjoy hiking, ask them what their favorite spots are or if they have ever had a scary experience hiking. It's great if you're also interested in the same things, but if not, you could even open yourself up by admitting your own fears about the topic, saying you could never do what they do. That would allow the other person to explain why they enjoy it so much or how they overcame the same fears.

Now, how about this scenario? You walk up to someone you mildly know and ask them how they're doing. They respond simply with "Fine" or "Things are going well," then proceed to ask how you are. You tell them you're doing okay as well. Cue the crickets. What happens now? There's no need to take a sudden interest in the ceiling texture. You don't even need to think of something interesting about your own life to talk about; think of what you can ask about theirs. First, think back to your previous interactions with this person. What was happening in their life the last time you saw them? What interests have they brought up in the past? Have they read the latest installment of the books or movie series they were obsessed with? Maybe you recall them mentioning a personal matter; ask them how that's going or what's new in their work or family. If nothing comes to you, use the trusty line, "What have you been up to lately?" It's an open-ended question that will cause them to think of an answer.

Now, once they respond to that question, or anytime someone makes any kind of statement, you have two choices. You can either let the conversation die a painful death by nodding silently when they've finished speaking or keep things moving by asking another question that prompts them to continue. Knowing what questions to ask will vary greatly from one setting to another, but regardless of the type of conversation, something you can always do is: *look for what's missing*. In the last chapter, you learned about re-engaging, so that your focus is on the person in front of you and how you can better understand what they're trying to tell you; not on how *you* are feeling and what *you* will say next. This is the key to knowing where to go next in a conversation, and when you refocus your attention, you can easily spot what's missing from what others have told you. A person often gives the minimum necessary information— likely because they don't want to bore others with too many details, either— and it can leave parts of their story unclear. You may automatically fill in the blanks in your mind and make some assumptions about what they're trying to say, but what if you used those blanks as an opportunity for more discussion? If you ask a friend what they've been up to, and they reply that they're "still working on a presentation for work," the implication is that they've been at it for a long time. Instead of just nodding and trying to think up a new topic of discussion, ask yourself what you don't understand about what they just said. How long have they been working on this project? What is the presentation about? Do they have an idea that will be a help to their company? Is it something they're really excited about, or is this a dreaded task that they can't get out of? Don't assume anything; ask them about it, and give them a chance to explain this part of their lives. Over time, they will come to understand that asking them what they've been up to isn't just something you like to cross off your conversational checklist, but that you're truly interested in them.

CHAPTER 5
ENDING A CONVERSATION

Well, bye.

You already knew that conversations can be hard to get into, but they can be really awkward to get *out of*, as well. No conversation lasts forever, so the ending of it is inevitable, but you want to bring the conversation to a close in a way that feels positive. Now that you've started a discussion and kept it going for a while, we'll talk about how to come in for a landing without ending things awkwardly or coming across as rude.

WHEN YOU'RE SHORT ON TIME

You shouldn't feel guilty for having time restraints. Often, people are waiting for you at home, your work break is almost over, or you're about to be late for class. You can't ignore other responsibilities in your life because you're in a conversation.

Let's say you've done such a great job in striking up a conversation with someone and putting them at ease that the conversation has gone really well. In fact, it has gone on for much longer than you expected, and now you're in danger of becoming late for your next appointment. But the person you're talking to is in the middle of a story. How do you get them to wrap it up without seeming rude or uninterested? Do you just interrupt them and say you need to get going? Do you wait for them to finish and risk being late?

First of all, if you know you have a time restraint, it's much better to avoid this situation from the beginning by mentioning that you're low on time and will need to get going soon *at the very start*. Try starting the conversation with something like:

- "Before I have to leave…"
- "I don't have long, but I wanted to ask…"
- "I've got to watch the time, but I was wondering…"

Using phrases like this lets the person know going into the conversation that you'll have to wrap it up shortly due to time constraints. That way, it's expected and understood when it happens, and no feelings are hurt in the process.

You can also do this mid-conversation when it's your turn to speak. As they finish what they're saying, you can respond with, "That's great. Hey, I'm going to have to run, but real quick…" followed by a closed question. This will keep the conversation from ending too abruptly but also keep it from dragging on, as it would with an open question. It would sound like this:

"That's great. Hey, I'm going to have to run, but

real quick, do you think you'll be at the meeting next week?" "Yes, I should be there." "Great, we can talk about this more then. In the meantime, text me any details you think I might need."

Setting time restraints early can actually work to your advantage. When people know that you're only there for a short, set period of time, they tend to get to talking more quickly.

If you have introduced a time constraint, but now the conversation is going so well that you lose track of time or are having a tough time ending the talk, the other person may actually be the one to remember your need to leave. If they say, "Wait, didn't you have to go meet your friend?" You may be tempted to tell them, "Nah, go ahead and finish your story," in an effort to be polite, but this will likely backfire on you, and it will be harder to leave later on. Instead, accept the offer in a nice, even complimentary way. You could say something like, "Oh, thanks so much for the reminder. I completely lost track of time," or "I got so lost in the conversation that I almost forgot."

It's harder when the person is continuing to talk, and you can't get a word in to say that you need to go. In this situation, it is necessary to go ahead and interrupt, just do it as politely as possible. At some point, speak up and say, "I'm so sorry to interrupt you, but I just realized what time it is. I really have to go to catch my ride, but it was so nice to talk with you." You could add, "I hope I can hear the rest of that story next time," but only if it's true. In fact, the next time you see that person, a perfect start to your next conversation would be, "So tell me what happened with that situation you were telling me about."

UNAWKWARD WAYS TO WRAP IT UP

Time constraints aren't the only reason to end a conversation. You may find that the conversation you're in isn't really going anywhere, you may find the person rude and not want to continue, or you may simply have more people to say hello to.

One technique is to give yourself an out (Southern Living Editors & 2020, 2022). In the party setting, you might do this by saying you're going to grab another drink and asking the person you're talking to if they'd like one as well. Or, if you're trying to leave the party, you can say, "I'm on my way out, but it was great seeing you. We should hang out sometime soon."

When you're making an exit out of a conversation, be sure to offer an honest excuse as to why you're leaving. Lying is seldom a good idea, especially if you're found out. What if you tell someone that you're leaving a party, but that same person finds you at that same party an hour later? Well, they would understandably say, "Hey, I thought you were leaving?" which would make things a bit awkward for all involved.

Alternatively, you could give the person you're talking to an out. If you're talking to the host of that party, for instance, you might say, "I know you have a lot of guests, so I'll let you go, but I just wanted to say hi." This works doubly well if it's a special occasion because then you can end that sentence with, "I just wanted to say happy birthday/congratulations/etc.!"

Closing the loop is a solid way to end a conversation, whether you're talking in person or online. (Southern Living Editors & 2020, 2022). This essentially means to come back to where you started with the conversation. Say that it started with you telling the person that you know of them through your neighbor, Alice. It turned out that this person was quite good friends with Alice, so you said, "I'm amazed we never came across one another," or something similar. The conversation took off from there ("So, how did you and Alice meet," etc.). After talking for a while, you feel like it's time to end the chat. You can close the loop by saying, "I still can't believe you know Alice as well. She'll be so surprised when I tell her we met." This brings the conversation to a feeling of completion, so ending it there feels natural to both of you. No hard feelings, no fuss, and no muss.

Another option is to reference future plans. You could also say, "What do you think about all three of us getting together sometime? I can see if Alice is free this weekend." This could also be a great way of getting their contact information if you'd like to connect with them further in the future.

Finally, you could end a conversation using a couple of kind words. Let's say you're talking to someone, and you find yourself growing bored. It may not be their fault, maybe you're a little exhausted after a busy day, and you just want to go home and rest. Try paying the person a compliment, thanking them for something they suggested earlier in the conversation, or even for something they did in the recent past would be phenomenal ways of doing this. "Thank you so much for recommending that new pizza place. I'll have to give it a try," is one example. Or, "I really appreciate your taking the time to explain that assignment the other day. If there's ever anything I can do for you…" A sincere compliment and genuine gratitude could go a long way in most cases, especially when you're trying to end a conversation gently and kindly.

All of the previous examples should be followed by a closer. Just a brief way of saying goodbye; that will be the last thing you say to them before walking away. You've probably seen a comedy bit where two lovebirds are trying to end a phone call, and even though they've both said they have to go, they get stuck in a cyclone of, "No, *you* hang up. No, *you*." Do you know what those people need? That's right, a closer! Plan your closer now so that you can give it, then walk away without dragging things on and on. Some closing lines that you can add to the end of just about any conversation are:

- "It was great to see you; take care."
- "Let me know how things go, ok? Bye!"
- "Talk to you soon!"

And just like that, you're on your way, having the satisfaction of knowing you have stepped out of your comfort zone, struck up a conversation, carried it well, and ended it gracefully. Pat yourself on the back for a job well done! Just— not until you're out of everyone's line of sight.

Dealing with Hurdles

without getting tripped up

CHAPTER 6
WHEN IT DOESN'T GO AS PLANNED

Well, that was awkward.

ere's the thing: Human beings are not perfect. They make mistakes, forget things, drop the ball, and some are just plain rude. Not every conversation you have with people is going to go as well as you want it to. Please know that *that's OK!* Sometimes you'll get too nervous and say something that you'll end up berating yourself about later. Sometimes there'll be some sort of miscommunication between you and the people you're talking to, or you could even get into arguments or cause offense to others, whether you mean to or not. You'll catch someone on a bad day and not know why they're so short with you or distracted. When something does go wrong, don't get discouraged. While the inclination to get angry with them or criticize yourself is understandable, it's not helpful, and you need to remember that this kind of thing happens to all of us. *It's not you, it's everyone!* We're only human, after all. Luckily, such things can usually be remedied. It is possible to salvage a conversation or relationship after things have gone awry. You need only to know how.

BREAKING THE [AWKWARD] SILENCE

Sometimes, a conversation has started off well enough, but soon you struggle to come up with things to say. So does the person you're talking to. The gaps between the talking seem to get wider every time. Your palms start to sweat. You look around, maybe hoping something interesting will catch your eye and make for some topic of conversation. You start to fidget as your mind races. What are you supposed to say next? This is one kind of problem you could easily encounter in any conversation. You can have it with strangers whom you're just getting to know. Long-time friends can reach a lull in the conversation when one drifts off, deep in thought. As a matter of fact, this one issue is so common that it can be what intimidates people the most about talking to people.

First, let's start by taking a deep breath. You need to be okay with silence at times. Not all silence has to be awkward silence. Many times, there is a natural ebb and flow in conversation, where there's excited chatter, then a lull, then it slowly picks up again. An example of this could be when a couple of moms have brought their children together for a playdate. The two of them may laugh about something their children did recently, and then the laughter fades as they go back to watching the kids play. After a while, one will mention something new, but neither of them was uncomfortable during the time it was quiet. Be comfortable enough with yourself and others that you can eat your meal or enjoy your surroundings without filling all the empty space with chatter.

Now, I understand that there are some silences that really are awkward. You can try to avoid these by **preparing things to talk about in advance**. This works especially well if you're going to a party, event, get-together, or meeting where there'll be people you don't know well. Of course, preparing things to talk about doesn't mean writing down little speeches on 3x5 cards that you carry in your pocket. Rather, it means simply reviewing some good questions or recent events that might be good conversation starters beforehand. Before arriving at your get-together, think about the things you did earlier that day or week. Did anything interesting happen that you could share with others? Did you run into a problem that someone at the party has experience with? Ask yourself, "What is one interesting thing that happened recently?" This way, you have an answer in mind when someone inevitably asks you something like, "So, what have you been up to?"

While you're at it, try to **think of three really good stories to share with people**. Again, this doesn't mean sit down and write short stories that you could read aloud (unless you're going to an open mic night, in which case, go right ahead). Maybe you saw something interesting/funny/concerning online or learned something new. All right then, take a couple of minutes to think of three stories you can share. Go on; I'll wait... Got them? Good. Now, the question is, how do you tell these stories in an interesting, engaging way? You do so by following these rules:

1. Don't include too many superfluous details. Nobody wants to know what model car you were driving unless it's relevant to the story you're telling. I've found myself falling into this trap many times. By the time you get to the relevant part of the story, your audience is so bored with the abundance of detail in the scene you have painted that they can't figure out which way the story is going. Get to the main points.

2. Specify who's in the story. If you keep talking about a "Mary" in your story and

fail to mention that Mary is your dog, the people you're talking to might assume she's a relative and thus become very confused when you say you got her "fixed."

3. Describe where you were when this event took place. Getting lost in the mall is understandably very different from getting lost in the woods with no cellphone reception.

4. Describe what obstacle or challenge you encountered. Every good story has one.

5. Describe how you got over the obstacle before you jump to the end. You don't have to elaborate more than necessary, but there needs to be a logical transition from Point A to Point B.

6. Have a clear resolution or end. What was the overall point you wanted to convey from your story? What was interesting or funny about it?

How might a story that's crafted by following these rules look? Let's take a look at an example from Jeff Callahan's *Become More Compelling* blog (2020):

My wife and I set out one morning to drive to a famous

waterfall in Iceland called "Gullfoss." We got in the car and set out. I checked all the gauges in the car, and I saw that the rental place had only given us 3/4 of a tank. No big deal, I thought. On the drive, we were blown away by the landscape. It looked like something out of a movie. The emptiness was immense. As we were driving along, I realized that the gas gauge in our car was the only gauge going from right to left. The rental place had actually left us with 1/4 of a tank, not 3/4. We'd been driving for a while, and Iceland isn't known for having gas stations every few miles. We pulled over and called the rental place while frantically spelling out Icelandic roads that we were near to see if there was a gas station nearby. They told us about a gas station about a half hour away. It wasn't on any map. At this point, our fuel light was on, and we had to keep driving further into inland Iceland. 30 white-knuckled minutes later, we rolled into the gas station on fumes. We barely made it.

Notice the details that Jeff *didn't* give. He didn't tell us why they chose Iceland as their destination, how much his wife loves waterfalls, or what the rental car shop was like. Those things may be relevant to another story about their trip, but they're not relevant to this one.

Think about the last time you shared a personal story with someone. Did you follow the rules laid out here? How might you change your telling of the

story to follow them better? You may want to practice a story that you could use in a future conversation. This might sound like an odd kind of rehearsal
to do, but stand-up comedians and public speakers
do this kind of thing all the time. So, if this is an area
you struggle with, it may help to make like a pro,
and practice. When you do this, you can be sure you
have stories to whip out if and when you feel like
you're running out of things to say.

One technique you can always use when silence
starts creeping in like this is what's known as **the
Spokes Method**. This method involves listening
"around" a topic that's being discussed for other
possible avenues of conversation. What exactly does
that mean? Picture a bicycle wheel in your mind. The
center of the wheel is the main topic you're
discussing. The spokes that extend out from that
center are sub-topics and observations related to that
topic, as well as questions you could ask about it.
Let's say that someone is telling you about a jazz
concert they just went to. You don't know much
about jazz; maybe you aren't very interested in it.
What are some of the "spokes" that are related to
jazz? You could ask what got them interested in jazz
in the first place or who their favorite jazz musicians
are. Another question might be about the Aretha
Franklin movie that came out recently. Did they

happen to watch that, by any chance? If so, what did they think? Or you could find out if they play any instruments or sing themselves. If so, do they play or sing any other kinds of music? Perhaps you could mention that you started learning an instrument as a kid, but eventually switched to sports. *Sports!* Now we've jumped to a whole new wheel and a new set of spokes! The possibilities can be endless because every topic can relate to another topic in some way.

Now, let's do a practice run. You're taking a tour of a college campus. The guy walking next to you says that he wants to study civil engineering. You don't know much about civil engineering. Can you find three spokes about it to start a conversation around it?

1.

2.

3.

Have you thought of any yet? Great! Here are a couple more examples that you could make use of in this scenario:

1. How did you first become interested in civil engineering?
2. How good is the civil engineering program at this school?

3. Is there any specific kind of project you'd love to work on as a civil engineer?

When you encounter a topic you don't know much about and risk encountering an awkward silence, start thinking *around* the topic. Ask yourself what the spokes about this topic might be, and you should be able to find at least one or two. You can then ask engaging questions or make unique observations that will keep the conversation flowing.

The final technique you can use to overcome silence is **asking digging questions**. Digging questions are ones that allow you to dig deeper into whatever subject you're talking about. Suppose you've found out that a classmate used to do ballet. If you ask them whether they liked it or not, they might simply respond with "yes" or "no" and move on. If you ask them questions that will prompt them to "dig deeper," however, you'll create more topics of conversation. Examples of this might be:

- How long were you involved in ballet?
- How did you get started in that?
- Did you enjoy it?
- Why did you stop?
- If you could go back, would you still take up ballet?

Questions and prompts like these add detail and deepen your conversation. They open up new discussion topics and allow you to get to know the other person on a more personal level. This may be the best bumper you can have against encroaching awkward silences.

KEEPING IT INTERESTING

A big communication obstacle, at least for most people, is fear. A lot of people are afraid of being boring. They're afraid that they're not interesting enough or have nothing significant to say during a conversation. Unfortunately, this fear makes them act less interesting than they actually are. They become so preoccupied with being interesting that they pretty much forget all the interesting things they do and could have shared with others. Have you ever walked away from a stalled conversation, only to think up a million different things you could have said rather than standing there, twiddling your thumbs? I'm sure you have, and I'm sure you've berated yourself about this. Don't. This actually happens to all of us. We all fear being uninteresting, and this fear results in our becoming less memorable, less impressive, less charismatic... In a word, just *less*.

You might think that the opposite of interesting is

uninteresting. But actually, according to Vanessa Van Edwards from the Science of People, the antithesis of being interesting is being *lazy* (Van Edwards, 2019)! This is because lazy people are lazy in everything they do, including making conversation. A lazy person might respond to the question, "How was your summer," with "It was fine." They might not even ask the person they're talking to how their summer was because they can't be bothered by it. This would hardly make for a fruitful conversation. A non-lazy person might respond with, "It was good. I spent a lot of time at the skatepark," or "I went to a summer program in New York, and it was so much better than I thought it would be." Then they'd follow that up with, "And how was your summer?" thus kickstarting a good conversation.

What this means is that the key to overcoming the fear of being uninteresting is to fight off your lazier tendencies. Don't just expect people to do all of the talking and entertain you. Be ready to do some of the talking yourself, actively listen, and—horror of all horrors—ask relevant questions! Of course, to be interesting in a conversation, you must have something interesting to share. If you're doing the same things every day—watching the same shows at the same time, eating the same dinner every night, etc.—then odds are, you won't have anything interesting to share with people. If you start trying new things, though, suddenly, you'll have lots of interesting things to talk about. Who knew, right? This doesn't mean you should suddenly get up and go base jumping. You can start small. That Mexican restaurant you've been meaning to try for ages but haven't gotten around to. Why not give it a go? Then tomorrow, when someone asks you what you were up to the other night, you'll be able to surprise them and say, "Oh, I went to that new Mexican place." This will likely prompt that person to ask how it was, to which you can respond with something like, "Oh, it was really good! You need to try their [insert menu item]" or "It was really bad. In fact, I think I got some food poisoning…" or anything in between. Now it's true that you can't do something new and interesting each and every day. However, you can try one new thing, be it a new hobby, restaurant, or TV show, every month. This way, you'll be regularly providing yourself with new topics of conversation that you can pull out when you need to.

As you've seen, being an engaging conversation-alist is as much about actively listening to others and asking questions as it is about sharing interesting things. If you show a genuine interest in someone and you're making an effort to contribute to the conversation, you will hardly need to worry about being bored, nor boring.

PREVENTING AND CLEARING UP MISUNDERSTANDINGS

No matter how good a conversationalist you are, misunderstandings happen. They are bound to. Human beings aren't perfect, as we've said.

I remember a time I tried to tell a group of people that I would have done great in Vaudeville if I had lived at the right time. Except I forgot the right word and ended up saying "Burlesque" instead of Vaudeville. When everyone (especially the women in the group) seemed to get uneasy, I figured they just didn't understand how much better my cheesy jokes would sound if I told them on stage in a suit and top hat. I had no idea they were trying not to picture me doing an R-rated dance in a 1920s getup. When I realized late that night that I said "Burlesque," I laughed until I cried and sent this message to everyone who had been present: "VAUDEVILLE! I meant Vaudeville!"

It happens. We misspeak, or something you say might mean something entirely different to someone else. You might struggle to get your point across because of nerves, leaving the other person unsure of what to think. Misunderstandings are inevitable, but they don't have to be game-stoppers— at least not if they're handled correctly. For the most part, misunderstandings can fit into two main categories; those that cause confusion and those that cause offense. Of course, there will be some overlap, but they will primarily be one type or the other. Both types, however, can be corrected and overcome. But before we can dive into what you must do to fix them, we must first go over what you absolutely *mustn't* do. This, luckily, is a very short and easily remembered list:

- Do **not,** under *any* circumstances, ignore a misunderstanding.

That's it. That's the only thing you really **shouldn't** do when a misunderstanding takes place. If you think that letting time go by will ease the tension or playing it off like nothing happened with make people overlook it, you're wrong. Completely wrong. The confusion or offense only builds as time goes on.

Let's look first at misunderstandings that cause confusion. My burlesque debacle was a good example of one of those. This type can happen when things are lost in translation or when one person misses a small part of the conversation. You think you are *basically* still following the conversation, so you don't ask for clarification. Let's say, for example, the person is describing the day they had with Toby. The story makes sense and all; it just seems like the way they treat Toby is a little harsh, making him eat outside and whatnot. You get more and more upset about how they're talking about Toby until they mention getting him getting his rabies shot, and you realize that Toby is a dog.

So you can see that miscommunication doesn't only happen because the speaker doesn't say something right, but also when the listener doesn't hear something right. If you notice that you're talking to someone who's distracted or preoccupied with something, there's a good chance that some information will be missed or misunderstood, and it may not be a good time to discuss something important.

Sometimes these misunderstandings can be humorous, but most of the time, they lead to a lot of awkward fumbling that leaves you thinking, "What's the matter with me?" the rest of the day.

If you're a fan of the TV show, The Office, you may remember an episode where two of the main characters, Jim and Pam, are talking on the phone. Pam is at the office, and Jim is out of town, and they both miss each other but aren't sure if the other one does. Of course, a lot of misunderstandings could have been cleared up if either one of them had been honest about their feelings, but neither one wanted to do that. They pushed through the uneasiness at the beginning of the conversation and started having a great time chatting and laughing together. That came to a halt when someone walked past Pam to go home, and Pam said goodbye to them. Jim, on the phone, thought she was saying an abrupt goodbye to *him*, and he was embarrassed for rambling on when she apparently wanted to get off the phone. *Right here*, it could have been cleared up if Pam had said, "No, I was saying goodbye to someone that's here, not to you." But when she tried, Jim interrupted, so she let it go. The two fumbled around, mumbling things like, "Oh, right, I should probably go—" They got off the phone with awkward embarrassment on both sides, which lingered for a long time.

It helps to see such a scenario played out in front of our eyes onscreen because it's so easy to see what went wrong and what they should have done to fix it. *"Just tell him what happened!"* I shout at the TV. Although I know that if it were me in that scenario, I, too, would have the impulse to play off any confusion so as to avoid looking stupid. Why do we do this to ourselves? Sometimes I think that "playing it off" and trying not to look stupid gets us into more trouble than anything else. It makes the situation worse and sometimes causes the very thing you fear; looking stupid, feeling uncomfortable, etc. I advise you, in the strongest way possible, that when you can sense that someone took what you said or did wrong, address it head-on, whether you caught it immediately or if time has gone by. You could say, "I realized that we last spoke, I said something really odd, and I wanted to clarify." No matter how uncomfortable it is to clear up the confusion, it's better than the discomfort that the confusion causes otherwise.

That brings us to the second type of misunderstanding, which offends someone and causes them to get angry or distance themselves from you. They might sit around, waiting for an apology that won't be coming, and, as a result, the two of you might stop talking to each other. Maybe the way they said something only made you *think* they were angry with you when actually they were thinking of something else entirely. None of these things would go very far if you just confront the issue directly. That can be a rather stressful idea, especially if you're one who tends to avoid conflicts. So, how do you talk about a misunderstanding without making it worse?

First, you have to recognize that it happened. You'll start to sense that something is off between the two of you, and tension starts to build. But from there, you'll need to figure out what exactly went wrong. Oftentimes, you'll notice when something is taken wrong because the person may look taken aback or confused. If you know what it was, just go back to it and say, "You know, I don't think I said that very well. Let me try to explain." If it was something that they said that bothered you, try saying, "Can I stop you for a second? I think I missed something..."

If you don't know why tension is building, however, it's can be harder to confront. You just start to feel like this is no longer going very well. You wonder, *'Is there something in my teeth? Did I laugh when they weren't trying to be funny? WHAT?'* You'll want to power through, ignore the awkwardness, and wrap up the conversation to get out of there, but it would be far better if you would pause right then and say something like, "I feel like I said something wrong, is something bothering you?" It will either give you a chance to explain, or they will reassure you that everything is fine and you can continue.

GETTING HEATED (AND KEEPING YOUR COOL)

We've talked about how to work through some obstacles, but how about landmines? A landmine can be anything— a political stance, a religious belief, a personal decision, putting pineapple on pizza… you get the idea. There are as many different opinions in the world as there are people. So, it's only natural for us to disagree with one another. Being able to agree to disagree and not let our differences mar our relationships can be tricky. But with patience and practice, you'll be able to not only *keep* a relationship through disagreements, but you can even *enjoy* the time you spend talking to those with whom you disagree.

The method is the same whether it's you that's upset, the other person, or both. But it's more difficult to take the proper steps when you, yourself, are angry because you have to fight through the emotions and desire to be vindicated in order to take these steps at all. Healing a relationship is worth the work, and the only true way out of a conflict is through open communication.

Bring calm. The first objective is to bring a sense of calm to the situation. It's worth mentioning at this point that the way to do this is actually *not* to tell the other person to "calm down." You do not want to say that, ever. Ever, ever. Have you ever wondered why telling someone to calm down has such a volatile effect? The phrase essentially tells the person that they're overreacting and what they're upset about doesn't matter as much as they think it does. Even if that's true, telling them so is very insulting. So instead of saying those exact words, you're going to model the behavior, which will keep you calm, as well as them, as they naturally mirror and feed off your behavior.

First, take a deep breath. Deep, slow breaths really can calm you physically, evidenced by your slowing heart rate. So, give yourself a moment (or two) to slow things down and collect yourself. Remember that a lot of hurtful things might be said in the heat of the moment when your words are being fueled by anger or frustration. By taking a couple of moments to regroup, you can cool down and minimize the effect of your emotions. If your thoughts are whirling, try grounding yourself by staring at a specific object in the room as you take your deep breaths. Try to relax your posture as much as possible by keeping your hands loose and unclenched and your jaw slack. Roll your shoulders back. If possible, take the conversation to a seated position if there are chairs nearby, as this is an altogether less aggressive posture than standing. As you adjust your stance, body language, and tone of voice to support a calm discussion, the tension will ease on both sides. This is true for a couple of reasons. First, people tend to match the tone and volume of the ones speaking to them, and it is much harder to yell at someone when they're not yelling at you back. Secondly, your response shows them that you care about them. Instead of lashing back at them with an emotional knee-jerk reaction as they might have been expecting, you have already begun to take time and energy to hear them out, and knowing this will help to put them at ease.

Keep resolution as the goal. Why would you go to so much trouble to make someone feel better when they're in your face? It's simple. Because people and relationships are more important than the issues that upset us. Too often, our true intention is to make someone feel the weight of what they did, to make our feelings understood, or make ourselves look better— no matter the cost. But your mission is to remember that fixing the relationship is more important than being right, so your goal must be to resolve the problem, not to win an argument.

Strive to understand. In order to resolve a problem, you have to understand it, correct? Too often, though, we assume we already understand the situation just fine; it's the other person who needs to understand things better! But as some wise philosopher once said, "You don't know what you don't know." Your teachable attitude from Chapter 4 is very important here. You must not allow arrogance to convince you that you already know everything you need to know and there couldn't be anything you haven't thought of. If someone has come to you upset, you need to give them a chance to get all their grievances out. Resist the urge to jump in and argue; just let them vent. Ask clarifying questions anytime something is unclear. When they come to a stopping point, respond first by acknowledging their feelings or intentions ("I'm so sorry things happened this way, you must be so hurt."), then ask questions that repeat back to them what you believe they're telling you. For example, "So, what you're telling me is that you feel [insert emotion] because when you saw [this] happen, you believed it was because of [that]. Is that right?" or "Do I have it right that when you said [insert quoted words], you meant [insert claim]?" By asking questions like this, you can immediately diffuse much of the aggravation the other person feels just because they know you're hearing them and trying to understand them. It will also help you to avoid further miscommunication from taking place, at least on your end.

When you're the one who is upset and confronting someone, you have the advantage that you're in control of the angry party, but also a disadvantage because you may be less rational when it's your emotions that are raging. Now, I'm going to take a wild guess that most of this book's audience is more introverted and less likely to confront people in anger. You may be more likely to stuff and stifle your anger, but it's still there, and you still ought to learn to deal with issues in a healthy, assertive way. In this case, your first objective is still to establish calm, but since you're the person initiating the confrontation, you're able to ensure that it's calm from the beginning. You can ask the person to sit and talk versus berating them in a doorway. You can set the conversation up for success, already having decided that you don't just want to chew the person out for what they did; you want to have a discussion to resolve a problem between you. What can you do to strive for understanding in this case since you can't make the person you're upset with ask you clarifying questions? You can do everything possible to be clear in what you have to say. It might be helpful to write out what you want to talk to your friend about before you speak to them. What is the core message you're trying to convey? Do you understand what happened, or do you need to spend more time looking to evaluate it or ask people some questions? You don't need to read what you've written to your friend, but this exercise can clarify what exactly you're experiencing and why the people involved have acted the way they have. Once you have clarity, you can have that talk with your friend without as much stumbling, confusion, or raw emotion.

You'll still begin talking with the person by acknowledging their feelings or intentions. "You're a good friend, and you probably didn't mean anything by this, but..." Of course, when something has upset you, you believe you're right because your mind and emotions are all screaming that you have been wronged. But you can't solve or de-escalate an argument if you're trying to get the last word in and "win." That won't help resolve anything. It won't even help you to communicate what you're feeling and experiencing. So remember to practice humility and phrase your statements into opportunities for clarification. "It seems like you deliberately lied to me about this to use it for your advantage, but maybe I'm missing something here." Give the person a chance to explain their side of the situation, and from there, you can gauge their honesty and true intentions.

Let's see this play out in the case of a missed deadline. Say a friend of yours filled you in on a class you missed and told you everything you needed to know about an upcoming assignment that was discussed in the class. You were glad for the help, but when you turned in the assignment, you found that it was due the day before, and being late cost you your grade. You're upset. There was a lot riding on that grade, and missing the due date wasn't your fault. *If they had told me the dates correctly,* you're thinking, *this wouldn't have happened.* You might be right, or you might be wrong. After all, we don't know why the miscommunication happened yet. Either your friend poorly relayed the information you needed, or it was poorly relayed to them, or you didn't listen as well as you should have. Like it or not, those are all possibilities, so pointing fingers won't help you at this point; you need more information. Actually, pointing fingers wouldn't help you, even if the fault rested solely with your friend. When you make accusations, you're only communicating anger and blame rather than how it affected you. There is no resolution in this. It causes your friend to react defensively. They feel attacked, and they attack back. After all, your friend was only trying to help you when they told you about this assignment, weren't they? They might believe you misheard them when they were trying to help, and now you're blaming them when it goes wrong. So, they might be hurt by this and react in anger, just like you.

You want to avoid the scenario where you keep attacking each other until you're in a shouting match, and one of you storms off, so you decide to try to model calm behavior. You relax your body, ask your friend to talk for a minute, and start by saying, "I know you were only trying to help." or, "I appreciate what you were trying to do," before explaining why your assignment was late. You ask a few questions to find out if she had the date correct, to begin with. Perhaps in the end, your friend is able to speak to the professor on your behalf, and he cuts you some slack, or maybe what's done is done, and you have only to forgive your friend. But you've had the chance to express yourself in a way that didn't damage the relationship between you and your friend, and they have also learned an important lesson about relaying accurate information.

Hard cases. These techniques work, and I have personally seen them resolve conflicts in the most unlikely of circumstances, but there will be exceptionally hard cases. You may deal with someone who is absolutely belligerent and irrational, or you might be the one so angry you can't see straight. Situations like these can make one or both of you want to flee, as though your fight or flight response has been engaged. It's important not to give into the urge to run away when it strikes during an argument, though. Doing so could make the other person feel as though you don't care about their side of things and you're not interested in hearing them out; you only want to be angry. This can fuel the fire and make the situation—and subsequently your relationship—worse. So, try to refrain from walking away from arguments unless you're in physical danger. If you feel genuinely unsafe during an argument, the logical thing to do is to leave. Always. If that's not the case, though, try to stick with the situation. If you've tried repeatedly, but they refuse to be calmed, or if you cannot get your own anger under control, excuse yourself to leave by saying, "I need some time to calm down. I'll talk to you about this another time." This is not the same as running away, mind you. You're not leaving things up in the air unresolved. You are hitting pause for a while so that you can collect your thoughts, come back, and pick up the conversation when you're in a better frame of mind. Doing this can be incredibly helpful in that it'll prevent quick, fiery emotions from directing the conversation. If you do put the conversation on hold, it will be important to prepare for the next conversation beforehand. Think through what some of the issues were that you had the last time you talked. Was there some misunderstanding they kept repeating that needs to be explained? Aside from anger, what were they really feeling or struggling with? Maybe under all their rage, they were actually worried or humiliated. Is there anything you can do to ease that? As you're considering these questions, try to explore points of view other than your own. You may also be able to identify what caused you to react so angrily as well. How can you begin the next conversation that will diffuse some of these emotions on both sides? You may also consider what the best time and place would be to talk to your friend the next time. Right before a stressful event or when you're pressed for time would be poor timing. Would it be better if you found somewhere nice and quiet to talk, where you wouldn't be interrupted? Even offering to buy them coffee when you meet could be a gesture of goodwill that will point steer the conversation toward reconciliation.

When you are having tough conversations like these, try to be as open as you can be. This means being very conscious of how you communicate and choosing your words carefully rather than letting quick-fire emotions, like anger, dictate them. Try to be aware of your tone, as well. Saying "I'm sorry" in a sincere tone is bound to have a very different effect than saying it curtly, with a twinge of irony.

When your friend is talking to you, actually listen to them and show it by saying "I understand" or "I hear you" when they explain what's bothering them. Try to hear your friend's pain points as they talk. These are things that communicate hurt, pain, and fear—things they might have felt during your argument or in an incident that led to that argument. For instance, the fear of losing a friend can get people to act very cold and unpleasant. If your friend is saying they reacted a certain way because they were afraid of losing you, then you need to actually hear that. Otherwise, how can you address the incident that caused your friend to become swept up by that fear? How can you prevent it from happening again? In keeping with that, try to be non-judgmental as you listen. Their reasoning may seem absurd to you, but it's very real to them, so don't roll your eyes and respond with, "Oh, don't be ridiculous; you wouldn't *lose* me as a friend." Remember that when people explain their feelings or fears, they're sharing perceptions, not facts. If a friend says they're worried they might lose you, they would need reassurance, not correction.

What if the conversation becomes heated again, and you need another pause? That's perfectly fine. Resolving arguments can take time. So, be sure to give yourself that permission, but make your exit gracefully. Make it clear that you're not avoiding the conversation; you're just giving the two of you the time you both need to process things and calm down. You might say something like, "Thank you for telling me that. I need some time now, though, to think about what you've said." You might also say something like, "I value what you have to say, but I'm having a tough time hearing you at the moment and need to come back to this once I've calmed down a little." You may even end things with something like, "I really care about you as a friend, but I'd like to agree to disagree on this matter." Then you can calmly make your exit and revisit the issue if and when you feel you both are ready to.

CHAPTER 7
IMPROVING YOUR CONVERSATIONS

Does it ever get any better?

ABSOLUTELY.

f you have made it this far in the book, let me assure you that your communication skills have already improved by leaps and bounds. You won't feel like it until you get some practice, but as you're faced with various situations, you'll be amazed by what comes back to your mind that you can implement. We've talked about how to start conversations, carry them with interest, and navigate obstacles. All these instructions and suggestions may seem overwhelming right now. So many things to remember. But being a good conversationalist is not about a checklist of things to say and do; it's about caring enough to get to know and understand people. All of these principles work together to navigate human behavior, and they really will come more naturally and easily as you put them into practice. Here are a few key principles that are worth stating (or restating) that can help you be more convincing in discussions where there are disagreements and to have a greater impact in any conversation. (Headlee, 2016):

- Truly pay attention during a conversation. Listen to others more than you speak. Yes, this has been said numerous times in this book, but ask yourself, are you really a good listener, or do you just pretend to be? Knowing the signs that show you're paying attention to someone is helpful, but let's be honest; you wouldn't need to prove you are paying attention to someone if you are actually paying attention to them. All those signs that we discussed would already be evident in your body language, tone of voice, and the kinds of questions you are asking. Keep re-engaging your focus when necessary. Don't multitask; meaning don't mess with your phone while someone speaks. What if you find yourself disagreeing with something the two of you are discussing? It's even *more* important that you really pay attention to what they're saying. Don't start drafting counterarguments or objections in your head. Try to understand their perspective. Odds are, the person you're talking to will reciprocate this behavior and attitude in kind.

- Don't monologue. Yes, it's important you get your point across. But your point shouldn't take up the entire conversation. If it does, then the person you're talking to will become frustrated, just as you would if you were in their position. Keep your points as concise as you can, and stop yourself when you notice you're starting to ramble, yielding the floor. You can pick it up again later.

- Be teachable and humble. Bill Nye has said, "Everybody you will ever meet knows something you don't." Keep this in the back of your mind going into any conversation, even ones with people you fundamentally disagree with. You can always learn something, and why should you waste that opportunity?

- Ask good questions. Use open-ended and clarifying questions during conversations. You'll gain information, discover new ideas, and understand people so much more. Questions are the key to creating a fruitful, productive kind of dialogue.

- Don't fake it till you make it in conversations. Tell people when you don't know the answer. When you feel the need to "play something off," or save face, take that as a signal to stop and bring it out into the open instead. This might feel counterproductive, but consider this: What happens when you claim to know something you really don't? Does powering through an awkward statement make it go unnoticed? Fix the issue immediately, while it's the smallest.

- Don't assume everyone has the same experience as you. People end up with different opinions because they have very different life experiences from one another. In keeping with that, don't equate your experience with theirs. If someone states a strong emotion about something, don't just jump in right away in agreement, as if you already know exactly what they mean. They may have strong feelings based on something you haven't considered or could relate to. So give them a chance to express themselves, then be respectful of their views.

- Don't try to promote yourself during conversations. Yes, you might be very excited or enthusiastic about something, but ask yourself, "Is this really the right moment and the right way to share this?" Also, consider what value this information will add to the conversation. Most of the time, the answer to that question will be "none." That doesn't mean that you should never tell your friends about something great that happened to you; just keep it in balance so that you're not going on and on about yourself and bringing up the accolade at every opportunity. If you sense you may have talked about yourself a little too long, acknowledge it with a disclaimer such as, "Sorry guys, I'm probably talking about this too much, I'm just really excited about it."

- Don't give unnecessary details, especially if you're sharing a story. Nobody needs to know the exact date you won the championship game or what time the match took place. Those kinds of details will be boring for your listener. Take them out of the exciting story you're about to tell. I mean, think back to history class. Were you more interested in how the battles that were fought and the victories were won, or did you have the desire to memorize when and where those battles took place?

One of the best ways to improve your communication skills can, unfortunately, be a little tough to swallow, and that is through others' feedback. You can take a proactive approach and ask people close to you if they think you're a good listener, talk about yourself too much, come across as rude, etc. But in reality, you may get that kind of feedback when you don't ask for it. In that case, it will sting a little— no, a lot. It will sting a lot. But don't snap back with an insult of your own, do the same thing you would do in any other sort of confrontation. Calmly ask questions like, "What makes you say that?" and humbly apologize for coming across in that way. You can come a long way after this kind of criticism if you decide to grow from it and not be crushed by it.

SECTION FOUR

Let's Do This!

but then what?

CHAPTER 8
CONVERSATION TO CONNECTION

OK enough small talk already.

What does it take to go deeper?

Emotions

Desires

Trust

Everyone needs a good friend. Someone to walk through life with whom we know we can lean on when things get tough. We need friends who will be genuinely happy for us when we achieve something and who we enjoy spending time with. Building up friendships and relationships like this takes time, though. They don't just happen in a day. They happen over months and years through countless conversations— conversations that initially start out as small talk with strangers, which you now know quite a bit about. Over time, you get to know people better, bit by bit. Small talk slowly deepens, and with each passing conversation, you will know and understand the person before you more and more. Such conversations can help you improve your relationships, build a safe, solid support system, and network effectively. So, how do you take those conversations and transform them into deeper talks that forge real bonds? How can true friends be made from new acquaintances?

PRESENCE

The secret to connection isn't asking really deep and pointed questions. It's being fully present, in the moment with people, and listening to them attentively. A person needs to believe that you care about them before they will connect with you on a deeper level. When you give your full attention to the person you're talking to, *then* ask those questions that show them you want to understand more, you create a great deal of intimacy. And when you listen openly and without judgment, you create a safe space for them to talk to you and share more of themselves with you.

COMMONALITY

A great starting place to take an acquaintance deeper is to find common ground. Shared values, hobbies, and experiences can be an excellent foundation to build on. This goes far beyond the standard childhood question, "What kind of music do you listen to?" Rather, look for commonalities that matter to you. You may notice, whether on social media or in conversation, that you're both passionate about the same cause or you both enjoy antique shops or the same book genre. Discussing your differences is good, but when you find an area where you're really in sync, a sense of familiarity builds, and new opportunities for the two of you to grow closer are created.

SPENDING TIME

If you wish to connect more with a coworker, you'll have regular opportunities for conversation at work, but it probably won't go very far if you *only* see each other at work. A deeper connection happens when you spend time together in multiple contexts. Go out somewhere for lunch sometime, or attend a local event together on the weekend. Later, invite them into your home for a birthday party or just a casual night in. The more you see each other in different settings, especially ones where you're both relaxed and having a good time, the more you'll feel like you truly know each other and all your different sides. So break out of your comfort zone, and show some hospitality. Go check out the new restaurant together, or take your families to the same place for some fun.

GOING DEEPER

With what you've learned already, you're well on your way to building lasting relationships; you need only to allow the necessary time. But as you spend time with your new acquaintances around shared interests, you'll have more opportunities for discussions to go deeper. As time goes by, you're bound to run into good and bad times in your own life, as they are in theirs, and you'll have the chance to walk through those times together. Let's talk a little about taking the conversation between you to the next level.

First, we'll look at **emotion words** (Rodman, 2014). These are words that allow you to connect with people in a genuine, sincere way by describing the way you feel. Let's say you have a doctor's visit scheduled soon, and it's one that could bring you bad news. You may not talk to many people about it, but you feel like you'll go crazy if you don't talk to *someone* about it. Whichever friend you choose to tell about your upcoming appointment will likely be a closer friend after that conversation than they were before, if you're open enough to use some honest emotion words. Tell them how stressed and anxious you are about the appointment or that you're afraid of the test results. You could even tell them how silly you feel for worrying about it. Your friend will be able to connect with you on a heart level because these are all emotions that they have felt before. You've also given them an opportunity to comfort you and offer help— all things that strengthen your connection. Chances are, they will feel quite honored that you trusted them enough to confide in them.

Similarly, **desires** are vulnerable topics, and sharing your plans and dreams with someone implies trust and openness. If you're not sure they would be comfortable talking about what they want the most in life, start by telling them your own goals instead of asking about theirs. This will show them that you trust them enough to reveal what matters to you. Goals and dreams aren't always sensitive issues. Some people are thrilled to tell anyone who asks about their 5-year plan for their business. But others might be embarrassed to admit what it is they really want in life. Some could be dealing with infertility and can't think about the future without seeing the empty seats at their table. It would be a difficult thing for them to open up about this to just anyone. Whatever a person decides to reveal to you, be sure to react respectfully, as you would want them to react to your dreams.

I remember, as a teenager, talking with a friend who had taken dance classes for years. Before we graduated high school, she talked about her plans to get a job as a dancer at a certain mouse-themed park and also on a cruise ship so she could travel the world. I don't know why I thought that sounded so far-fetched, but being the thick-headed kid I was, I laughed and said something like, "And I'll be a rock star." (It was obvious that I had no real expectation of becoming a rock star.) Well, sure enough, she danced in mouse-themed parades for several years, then cruised the world as a dancer for many more years. She became a highly-sought after choreographer and has made a host of other accomplishments. I've always been amazed that she had such clear plans at a young age and sought them out. Every big name you read about in the news started out as someone with a wild idea. So don't be as short-sighted as I was. Believe in the dreams of those who share them with you. Who knows, maybe you can even play a role in helping them reach their goals.

Did you notice what sharing emotions and dreams have in common? Because they make you emotionally vulnerable, they both require **trust**. What greater element is there to a deep connection to someone than trust? As they say, it takes years to build trust and only moments to break it. The emotions and dreams we've discussed are very effective ways to build trust, but you must be careful not to lose it. Of course, you will lose someone's trust by being dishonest. Also, by laughing at them— even making light of their ideas or preferences. However, you can also break their confidence without intending to. Simply sharing information about them while making conversation with someone else can hurt your friend if they don't want it to be made public. The trick of it is you may not always know when something is too personal to share with others.

The safest rule of thumb is simply not to share anything about another person that isn't already public knowledge unless they have given you permission to share it. If your friend just got engaged, don't talk about their wedding until a formal engagement announcement has been made. If you know they plan to change jobs, don't mention it until they give their two-week notice. They may mention it to people before it's made public, but that is their decision to make, not anyone else's.

If sharing true and positive information about someone can be damaging, imagine the havoc you can cause by gossiping. Just don't do it. If you already tend to gossip, start working now to break the habit. Gossip is one of the fastest ways to destroy trust in a friendship. It really doesn't benefit you to gossip except to get a cheap laugh from others and to fill a void in a conversation. Decide now to use humor and fill conversations in ways that don't hurt other people.

Not only is gossip hurtful to the one you're talking *about*, but it isn't helping the relationship with the person you're talking *to*, either. After a while, they'll begin to wonder, *Do they gossip about me like this as well?* This suspicion stays in the back of their minds whether they realize it or not. It makes their coming to you with any kind of vulnerability a lot less likely. What if you betray their confidence and share it with someone else behind their back?

Instead of gossiping, try to praise mutual friends. Gossip is about tearing people down, even if they're not there to hear it. Praising people, on the other hand, is about lifting them up. As such, it evokes very different kinds of thoughts in the mind of the person you're talking to. When people hear you openly, willingly, and *genuinely* pointing out the good in others, they trust you. In turn, they become more likely to open up to you and share more of themselves with you, vulnerabilities and all— leading to meaningful conversations and strong, resilient relationships.

CHAPTER 9
LET'S REVIEW

I already forgot the first things you told me

Don't worry. Here's a recap…
pg. 153

T hroughout *How to Talk to People (And Not Feel Like an Idiot)*, you've learned many different strategies, techniques, and methods to start new conversations with people you've just met. You've discovered how to have small talk, how to express yourself clearly, and how to listen to others. You've seen the messages you can convey with your body language as well as how you can navigate heated arguments. Maybe you've even unveiled new ways to talk to people you disagree with and work together with them, as you inevitably will have to at some point in your life. Before we wrap things up, though, let's take a closer look at how we might put all that we have learned into practice. To that end, we'll be doing two things together. First, I'm going to give you a checklist covering everything we've gone through in this book. If you'd like, you can check over this list before going into an important conversation or intimidating social event that you're nervous about. It could help you remember points like your body language and handshaking skills before a job interview. Once that is done, you'll find a couple of exercises to do based on everything we've discussed.

THE CHECKLIST

• Have a confident mindset; who you've been in the past is not who you must always be. You add value to the conversation and others around you have value to share.

• Smile and keep your stance open and relaxed (such as by not crossing your arms).

• Lean forward/towards the person talking to you, and give them your attention.

• Use enough hand gestures as you explain your thoughts and experiences.

• Adopt a tone that's able to convey the emotions that you want to convey, such as confidence, excitement or understanding.

• Meet the eyes of the person that's talking to you for several seconds at a time.

• Shake the person's hand firmly with a smile and make eye contact.

• Choose a simple opening line. Don't try to be clever.

• Ask open-ended questions.

• Notice something about the person you're talking to and ask questions about it.

• When you receive answers, give feedback, then ask a follow-up question.

- In an online conversation, clearly express why you're reaching out to a stranger.

- If you already know the person you're talking to, reference something you've already talked about before.

- Read the room before you tell a joke. Is this the best/most appropriate moment for one?

- Attentively listen to others, and re-engage when needed.

- When someone is being vulnerable with you, try asking, "How can I help?" if you don't know how to respond.

- Don't try to cover your discomfort by making a joke.

- Don't put a lot of pressure on yourself to be funny. Remember, the best humor happens naturally.

- Open questions keep the conversation going.

- Closed questions help to clarify details or wrap things up.

- Don't stack questions.

- Keep your questions short and to the point.

- Give genuine compliments.

- Say "I don't know" when you can't honestly answer a question.

- Acknowledge your weaknesses and point out others' strengths.

- Give credit where credit is due.

• Don't be afraid to laugh and poke fun at yourself every once in a while.

• Always be respectful when talking to others.

• Express gratitude when talking about your own accomplishments.

• Don't monologue.

• Don't interrupt people when they're speaking to you.

• Ask clarifying questions when you need to.

• Physically focus on the person that's talking to you.

• Don't give unsolicited advice.

• Get details about interests, hobbies, likes, and dislikes.

• Have a good story to share planned ahead of time

• Don't make your stories too detailed.

• Use the Spokes Method to talk *around* a subject.

• Ask "digging" questions.

• Accept that misunderstandings will sometimes happen.

• Bring misunderstandings out into the open to be fixed.

• Understand what it is you want to and need to express.

• Don't let your anger do the talking for you.

• Give yourself a moment or two to calm down if

and when you need it.

• Don't point fingers, either literally or metaphorically.

• Model calm behavior.

• Acknowledge the other person's feelings and intentions.

• Ask clarifying questions.

• Leave if you feel genuinely unsafe or threatened in an argument.

• If you feel frustrated or overwhelmed, take a pause, with the understanding that both parties will revisit the conversation once they have calmed down a bit.

• Prepare for how you want to resume the conversation after the break.

• Try to explore the other person's perspective during the break.

• Identify your triggers during the break.

• Figure out the best time and place to resume the discussion.

• Come back to the conversation after a sufficient pause.

• Be as open as you can be when you come back to the discussion.

• Listen to what the other person is telling you.

• Take another break/pause if and when you need it.

- Try to do one interesting (new) thing per month.
- Don't be lazy in conversation.
- Ask follow-up questions that are relevant.
- Use "emotion" words.
- Don't gossip.
- Praise other people, even when they're not there.
- Don't interrupt people.
- Remember that everybody you meet knows at least one thing that you don't.
- Don't assume your experience is the same as another person's.
- Introduce any time constraints at the beginning of the conversation.
- Reintroduce the time constraint to the conversation in a kind, polite way if and when you're reminded of it.
- Offer to talk again when you have more time.
- Only use a real excuse to bail from a conversation.
- Give the person you're talking to an out.
- Close the loop as a way of ending a conversation.
- Reference future plans.
- Use kind words when you're ending a conversation.
- Say goodbye.

CHAPTER 10
PRACTICE MAKES PROGRESS

What's next?

That's it!

But I'm not ready.

"Ready" never comes.

But you ARE ready to practice.

W hew! That was quite the checklist, wasn't it? All of that probably feels like a LOT to remember. But see, this is why we practice. Thinking through a few scenarios can help to ease your mind because, unlike in the middle of a live conversation, you have time to think of a good way to resolve the situation. No matter how daunting a scenario may seem at first, you can always find a solution if you give it enough thought. The more you practice, both on paper and in person, the simpler each of these concepts will seem. You will find that, in time, you will be able to smooth over sticky social situations much more easily than you ever thought was possible.

CHANGING YOUR MINDSET

Scenario: You want to turn and talk to the person sitting next to you. But thoughts like *I'm not all that interesting* and *She wouldn't want to talk to me anyways* are running through your mind.

Exercise: Write down five negative thoughts that go through your mind in such moments. Next, right down their positive or, at the very least, neutral counterparts directly opposite them.

1.

2.

3.

4.

5.

Scenario: You have a bit of a defeatist attitude that's preventing you from talking to the coworkers/other students in your group project.

Exercise: List all of the negative thoughts you have that are keeping you from speaking up and talking to them more. Now list specific evidence you have that supports these thoughts. Be honest! Are you able to come up with any? Would a friend of yours agree that there is evidence to support your negative thoughts?

_____

_____

_____

_____

_____

_____

HOW TO TALK TO STRANGERS

Scenario: You're at a party where you hardly know anyone. You spot someone across the room that seems approachable. You want to start up a conversation with them. But what do you say?

Exercise: List five simple openers you can use:
1.
2.
3.
4.
5.

Scenario: You noticed that the person you have a crush on dressed up as a superhero for Halloween.

Exercise: What are five questions you can ask them about this interest of theirs?
1.
2.
3.
4.
5.

CARRYING ON A CONVERSATION

Scenario: You're out at dinner with a crowded group of friends and are sitting next to someone you don't know very well. You started a conversation with them by asking about their favorite cuisine. They said that it was Indian.

Exercise: What are three open questions you could ask now? Circle one of your answers, then write how the conversation might continue if from that question.

Open Questions:

1.

2.

3.

Conversation:

You:

Them:

You:

Them:

You:

Them:

USING HUMOR

Scenario: Your friend comes by to talk, and he's really upset. He may be getting a divorce, and he needs someone to talk to. As he's walking you through everything he's feeling, you start getting a little uncomfortable. What are you supposed to say? Do you take his mind off things by making a joke once he has stopped talking, give him advice, or ask him what he needs?

Exercise: Think of all the possible responses you might give in this situation. Write them down. If you were in your friend's position, how might you react to these responses? Write down how each of them would make you feel. Then write down how you'd want this scenario to go.

_____

_____

_____

_____

_____

_____

SHARING YOUR SUCCESSES

Scenario: You applied to your dream college and got in. You're excited and can't wait to share the news with your friends. But most of them are all still waiting to hear back on their college applications, and one that you know of just received a rejection letter.

Exercise: How might you share this good news with your friends without seeming to be bragging or insensitive? Write down at least three ways:

_____

_____

_____

_____

_____

_____

ENDING A CONVERSATION

Scenario: You've been talking to a semi-close friend, and the conversation seems to be droning on. You're a little bored, if you're being honest, and you just want to leave.

· · ·

Exercise: How might you end this conversation without coming across as rude or upsetting your friend? Write down at least three ways!

_____

_____

_____

_____

_____

_____

BREAKING THE SILENCE

Scenario: You've asked someone what they've been up to, and they respond that they just at spent some time at a lakeside cabin over the weekend.

Exercise: Think of some assumptions you might make about this person based on their statement. What information is missing? List 3-5 questions you could ask in response to clarify and understand them better.

_____

_____

_____

_____

_____

Scenario: You're about to head out on a first date. But you're worried that you'll have nothing to talk about.

Exercise: Write down five interests your date has (or that your friends have, if you don't *actually* have an upcoming date) that you don't know much about. What kinds of interesting questions can you ask about them? While you're at it, think of three interesting stories you could share. What would those stories be? How might you share them in an engaging way?

_____

_____

_____

_____

_____

_____

PREVENTING MISUNDERSTANDINGS

Scenario: Someone you know is waiting in a grocery store line in front of you. She turns around and starts talking to you. You chat for a while and laugh about different things. Suddenly, she looks a little surprised and stops responding in the same way. She smiles politely and gradually turns back around to face mostly forward. You wonder if you said something that bothered her but are afraid to ask.

Exercise: What should you say or do?

_____

_____

_____

_____

_____

_____

CALMING THINGS DOWN DURING AN ARGUMENT

Scenario: You have gotten into a tense argument with your friend because he has canceled your plans for the 3rd time in a row. This time, it costs you a significant amount of money. You feel as though your time and money are unimportant to him, and he seems to want anything besides hanging out with you. You can't seem to be able to communicate why you're this angry, though. Your friend gets angry in turn and keeps saying, "What's the big deal?" The more he acts like it's not a big deal, the angrier you become.

Exercise: How might you calm yourself enough to get to a place where you can communicate clearly with your friend in this situation? How would you explain the real issues that are bothering you?

_____

_____

_____

_____

_____

_____

AFTERWORD

Conversations can be a difficult beast to master, but as you have seen, it can be achieved with some fore-thought and the right mindset. As you go about each day, remember these basic principles of the art of communication:

- Have the confidence to speak up, knowing that you are worth hearing, and so are the others around you whom you can learn from.
- Show your confidence and interest in people with your body language.
- Keep your opening lines short and simple.
- Ask open questions that are relevant to what you're talking about when you want to keep a conversation going.

- Give feedback and tell stories concisely.
- Don't interrupt, brag, or use humor offensively.
- Always be respectful and end conversations politely.
- Finally, always, always, ALWAYS, listen to people attentively and without judgment.

As long as you keep these key points in mind, you'll be well on your way to feeling free and comfortable in social situations and developing meaningful relationships with the people in your life. In the meantime, you can always keep flipping through the pages of this book to get a refresher any time you need it. You'll be able to try out some of the exercises suggested on its pages and come up with your own. Put yourself out there again and again and start having different conversations with anyone that you can. Your friends, family, or someone in line at your coffee shop— challenge yourself to engage with one new person every day. Over time, you won't believe how comfortable you can feel when you talk to people (and *not* feel like an idiot)!

I hope you've enjoyed learning How to Talk to People (and not feel like an idiot). If you've found this book to be helpful and believe you can make use of some of the tools that it offers you, please take a moment to leave a review!

BIBLIOGRAPHY

Bennett, T. (2019, May 1). *What's the psychology behind humor? How can it help? Does it ever work against us?* Thriveworks. https://thriveworks.com/blog/whats-the-psychology-behind-humor/

Bergson, L., & Helgoe, C. (2019, November 21). *Body-language signs to watch when having a conversation.* Experience Life. https://experiencelife.lifetime.life/article/body-language-signs-to-watch-when-having-a-conversation/#:~:text=Leaning%20in%20indicates%20genuine%20interest

Brzosko, M. (2021, September 19). *How to have more meaningful conversations.* Medium. https://betterhumans.pub/how-to-have-more-meaningful-conversations-7b1f9120ff0d

Conversations that connect. The Professional Development Group. (n.d.). Theprofessionaldevelopmentgroup.com. https://theprofessionaldevelopmentgroup.com/article/2011-11/conversations-connect

Corcoran, J. (2014, April 11). *7 ways to brag without sounding like you're bragging.* Dumb Little Man. https://www.dumblittleman.com/7-ways-talk-accomplishments-without-sounding-like-youre-bragging/#:~:text=Here%20are%207%20ways%20you%20can%20be%20share

Cuddy, A. (2012, October). *Your body language may shape who you are.* Amy Cuddy. YouTube. https://youtu.be/Ks-_Mh1QhMc

Cuncic, A. (2020, May 1). *What is imposter syndrome?* Verywell Mind. https://www.verywellmind.com/imposter-syndrome-and-social-anxiety-disorder-4156469

Hailey, L. (2022, May 13). *How to talk to strangers like a pro (& avoid awkwardness)*. Science of People. https://www.scienceofpeople.com/talk-to-strangers/

Hanne Keiling. (2020, November 25). *Nonverbal communication skills: Definition and examples*. indeed.com. https://www.indeed.com/career-advice/career-development/nonverbal-communication-skills

Headlee, C. (2016, February 16). *10 ways to have a better conversation*. Www.ted.com. https://www.ted.com/talks/celeste_headlee_10_ways_to_have_a_better_conversation?referrer=playlist-the_art_of_meaningful_conversa&autoplay=true

Is your defeatist attitude keeping you down? Here's how to stop self defeating thoughts. (n.d.). Www.fingerprintforsuccess.com. https://www.fingerprintforsuccess.com/blog/defeatist-attitude#:~:text=A%20defeatist%20attitude%20is%20a

King, D. (2017). *How to maintain your cool when a conversation gets hot*. Final Touch. Final Touch School. https://finaltouch-school.com/civility/how-to-maintain-your-cool-when-a-conversation-gets-hot/

Me, K. I. (2016, April 26). *6 big costs of undervaluing yourself and how to build self confidence instead*. KeepInspiring.me. https://www.keepinspiring.me/how-to-build-self-confidence-undervaluing-yourself/

Mind. (2019). *Tips to improve your self-esteem*. Mind, the mental health charity - help for mental health problems. Mind.org.uk. https://www.mind.org.uk/information-support/types-of-mental-health-problems/self-esteem/tips-to-improve-your-self-esteem/

Mind Tools Content Team. (2009). *Questioning techniques: asking questions effectively*. Mindtools.com. https://www.mindtools.com/pages/article/newTMC_88.htm

Morin, D., & Wendler, D. (2022, August 30). *How to start a conversation (without being awkward)*. SocialPro. https://socialself.com/start-conversation/

[9 Tips] How To Keep A Conversation Going & Destroy Awkward Pauses. (2020, October 15). Become More Compelling. https://www.becomemorecompelling.com/blog/how-to-keep-a-conversation-going

Olsson, R. (2022, September 5). *4 Tips to de-escalate a heated argument.* Banner Health. Www.bannerhealth.com. https://www.bannerhealth.com/healthcareblog/advise-me/how-to-recognize-and-handle-a-heated-conversation

Rebecca. (2014, March 19). *Conversation Skills - How to END a conversation politely.* YouTube. https://www.youtube.com/watch?app=desktop&v=ce8u2OFrrXM&feature=youtu.be

Rebecca. (2021, January 11). *How to stop talking and listen more.* Minimalism Made Simple. https://www.minimalismmadesimple.com/home/how-to-stop-talking/#:~:text=How%20to%20Stop%20Talking%20and%20Listen%20More%201

Rodman, S. (2014, September 2). *10 ways to turn a conversation into a potential friendship.* Lifehack. https://www.lifehack.org/articles/communication/10-ways-turn-conversation-into-potential-friendship.html

Rubin, G. (2007, December 19). *Twelve tips to avoid seeming like an arrogant, know-it-all jerk.* HuffPost. https://www.huffpost.com/entry/twelve-tips-to-avoid-seem_b_77587

Sanders, V. (2021, September 24). *Actual Video From "Awkward to Awesome: The Art of Making Conversation."* SocialSelf. https://socialself.com/blog/become-more-approachable/v

SC. (2020, November 9). *How to use questions to help people think deeply (5:17).* Better Conversations. https://betterconversations.co/questions-to-think-deeply/

Sloat, S. (2021, March 21). *How to end a conversation: 2 science-backed methods.* Inverse. https://www.inverse.com/mind-body/ending-conversations-is-so-hard-study

Southern Living Editors, & 2020. (2022, August 8). *6 polite ways to end a conversation*. Southern Living. https://www.southernliv-ing.com/culture/how-to-end-conversation-etiquette

Spoelma, J. (2018, June 17). *Communication breakdown: how misun-derstandings happen and what to do about it*. Career Foresight Coaching. https://careerforesight.co/blog-feed/communica-tion-breakdown-how-misunderstandings-happen-and-what-to-do-about-it

The Josh Speaks. (2021a). *How To End a Conversation Without Being AWKWARD (Use This Trick!)*. YouTube. https://www.y-outube.com/watch?app=desktop&v=HXRD5I6n7rg&fea-ture=youtu.be

The Josh Speaks. (2021b). *When You Run Out of Things To Say, DO THIS To Keep a Conversation Going*. YouTube. https://www.y-outube.com/watch?app=desktop&v=XXbgdNc18W0&fea-ture=youtu.be

Van Edwards, V. (2016, January 12). *How to have and hold dazzling conversations with anyone: we review 11 science backed steps*. Science of People. https://www.scienceofpeople.com/have-hold-conversation/

Van Edwards, V. (2019). *How to be More Interesting*. YouTube. https://www.youtube.com/watch?v=xzvqkaSDJNs

Vanessa van Edwards, V. (2017, April 14). *How to Avoid Small Talk*. YouTube. https://www.youtube.com/watch?app=desk-top&v=9jZVbchb1Mc&feature=youtu.be

Vanessa Van Edwards. (2017). *You are contagious*. TEDxLondon https://www.youtube.com/watch?v=cef35Fk7YD8